8-5-76

THE GREATEST LITTLE GAME

8-5-76

THE GREATEST LITTLE GAME

A Complete How-to Book for the Coaches, Parents, Boys, and Girls in Kid Baseball

BY

MICKEY HERSKOWITZ AND STEVE PERKINS

SHEED AND WARD, INC.

Subsidiary of Universal Press Syndicate
New York

Library of Congress Catalog Card Number 74-10165

ISBN: 0-8362-0595-2 (cloth)
      0-8362-0626-6 (paper)

Contents

Preface

This work is about kid baseball, for the parents, coaches and kids who are involved in it. While The Greatest Little Game *is primarily intended as a how-to book, we have included sections on the history of kid baseball, a couple of the outstanding foreign teams of kid baseball, and brief biographies of two players who began in organized kid baseball and made it to the big leagues. In discussing these diverse aspects of the game, we hope to share our enthusiasm for the variety and richness of the game.*

The "Introduction" explains our biases about the involvement of kids in organized baseball and also contains a brief history of how this phenomenon developed.

Part I explains some of the skills and strategies of the game. We went to the pros, themselves, for tips on how to bat, pitch, and play the positions in the field. We think that these hints from the pros will help emphasize certain basics of the game. It's one thing for us to tell you how to improve your play as a catcher—it's quite another for Johnny Bench to tell you.

Part II is for the girls who play kid baseball. We think that, with the changing of attitudes, more girls will join the sport on an equal footing with boys. We address the problem of how girls can catch up and attain that equal footing, and provide some guidelines on how girls can develop baseball skills. If you're primarily interested in tips for girl players, this is the place to start reading the book.

Part III presents two separate stories, but stories which add much to the lore of kid baseball. One chapter tells of two pros who had their beginnings in kid baseball. These two professionals, Boog Powell and Joey Jay, are among the first graduates of organized kid baseball, and owe much to their early, formative training. The other chapter looks at a unique group of kid stars—the players on those foreign teams that so dominated kid baseball. We think their courage, determination and outstanding ability will be sorely missed in the coming years.

What we have tried to do is give enough of an idea of the fun one can derive from kid baseball. Its competitiveness, its action, its skills make it the greatest little game. For those who become involved in it—kids, parents, and coaches—it provides lasting rewards.

Introduction

The Kids Had to Play Someplace

A standing gag claims that kid baseball is a very good thing, because it keeps the parents off the street. There is a thread of truth to that, and critics of the program have pounced upon it. Over a period of years, in fact, it has become fashionable to knock kid baseball, to expose it as a corrupter of young egos, to repeat all manner of horror stories about eleven-year-olds warped by adult pressures and adult ambitions.

Certainly, the parents get in the way (that's why they're parents). Certainly, organized teams and leagues tend to regiment the youngsters and give them grown-up illusions. In no other nation are children so pampered and adults so vicariously thrilled. And with that said, another point cries to be made: The critics never seem to ask the kids. They *love* it. As kids always do, they find the fun and innocence in it. They thrive on the scale model big league world around them: ball park, bleachers, scoreboards, press boxes, p.a. systems. They cultivate the mannerisms ... the tap of the bat to knock dirt off rubber-cleated shoes, hitching the belt, rubbing rosin on their hands.

ix

The wonder of it is that anyone still bothers to attack organized kid baseball and what it represents. In terms of what else boys and girls today can get obsessed with—television, drugs, each other—it is clean, healthy and, yes, wonderfully old-fashioned.

And yet the critics can always seem to find a psychiatrist to decry the pressure it places on tender psyches and warn that to fail, to be excluded, can turn them into the kind of grownup who cries over empty gum wrappers.

Well, this book isn't for them. It is a celebration of kid baseball, not an indictment. The authors believe that it is time to quit kicking the tires, and accept the fact that the product runs. Petulance and adult temper, you see, are not limited to the grandstands of kid baseball. Or the dugouts. Herewith a story.

In what has become a classic example of managerial agony, Gene Mauch, then of the Phillies, watched his team blow a critical game in September of 1964 in Houston. It turned out to be more than just a game. It was the beginning of an historic collapse. The Phillies were to blow a 6½ game lead in the final weeks of the pennant race, dropping like a marble down a rainpipe. That night in Houston, Mauch stormed into his locker room to find his players already bellying up to the buffet table. With one mighty sweep of his arm, he cleared it—barbecued spareribs, cold cuts, watermelon slices, potato salad, all went flying in several directions, spattering the street clothes hanging in nearby lockers of two Phillie players. ("Boy," quipped one, "the food sure goes fast around here.")

What had been the immediate cause of Mauch's tantrum? "We got beat," he said, "by a guy who looks like a little leaguer." A bloop single in the last of the ninth by a baby-faced rookie named Joe Morgan had done in the Phillies. Morgan, it so happened, *had been* a little leaguer. He did not feel offended.

At this point, a distinction ought to be made between *baseball*, as practiced by the big fellows who get paid for it, and *kid baseball*, whose members play for the joy of it, and for the reflection in their mind's eye. This book is about the people and the teams who helped make it a national industry. There are tips and instructions on these pages, too, but their objective is to enable kids to play *their* game better—not to imitate the big fellows more closely. Too often, coaches absorb theories and techniques at clinics—where actual big leaguers demonstrate their art—and pass them on to youngsters unequipped, physically, to handle them, youngsters whose eagerness can only be defeated by failure.

This book is for the coach, parent, friend and fan who understands the purpose of such sport, who realizes that true competition is inside yourself: that is the essence of kid baseball. It is to be enjoyed, not to be analyzed. The American heritage in sport is to appreciate as much the good play muddled into, or the near catch well tried, as the good play properly done.

The folk heroes of baseball knew instinctively that the popularity and endurance of their sport rested in the very young. Not too many years apart, Babe Ruth and Ty Cobb—you can't get more folk heroic than that—addressed themselves to the very subject.

On his last visit to Yankee Stadium, his voice reduced to a hoarse whisper by the cancer that was killing him, Babe

Ruth urged the mamas and papas: "Start him when he's young, teach him to play baseball when he's four years old."

How Babe arrived at that age isn't known, but no doubt he simply considered three to be too immature.

When Ty Cobb, his own days numbered, took a final look around him at the game he loved, he, too, made a plaintive plea to young America: "Boys," he said, "strive to master the lost arts of a great game. Unless you dedicate yourself to that task now, as the old timers die off one by one, they will have vanished forever."

Ruth and Cobb and the guardians of the game knew something the critics cannot understand: that there was never a game more ideally suited to the soaring spirit, the boundless energy of the eternal child. "With a bat and a ball and his imagination," Branch Rickey once wrote, "a boy is a complete team."

Somehow we feel confident that Branch Rickey would have been delighted to know that, today, his statement would have to be expanded to read, "a boy ... or a girl ..."

After years of exclusion, the admission of girls into organized kid baseball was perfectly in tune with everything else in sports. The kid baseball player in pigtails today may have a college scholarship tomorrow. Although this book doesn't address instructions to a second baseperson there is a section focussing on girls, and the lessons throughout are valid for all the little people.

Branch Rickey understood kids and knew why they were important to baseball. He also knew why baseball was important to them, "Leisure is wonderful in creative hands," he said. "It accounts for great architecture, great paintings and great music . . . Leisure, however, is a damnable thing in the hands of an adolescent." No one ever spoke more lyrically about the game than Rickey, the man who invented the farm system, discovered Dizzy Dean, brought Jackie Robinson across the color line and never took a drink in his life, even though he once managed the St. Louis Browns.

To appreciate the full sweep of this game that little people play, you have to remember what the country was like before kid baseball began to develop. Yogi Berra, the great Yankee catcher, later the manager of the Mets, remembers: "When I was a kid we didn't have no lighted stadiums. We didn't always have nine to a side. We'd play with four kids, two on a side, and sometimes if we had only three we made that do, too. One would pitch, one hit and one shag. We'd do it for hours."

Kids who were lucky enough to have a lump of something that passed for a baseball, and maybe a broom handle for a bat, made do, too. But they could always get up a game, and there was never a problem finding a vacant lot. In the forties and early fifties, America was rich in vacant lots, the diamonds of our boyhood dreams. The great urban problem, the crisis of the inner cities to come, would change all that.

Organized kid baseball was a neighborhood idea that mushroomed into an American institution. Today it belongs to the landscape, the summer scene, as observed from the windows of passing cars and trains across the land.

It began with a $35 donation and an irrepressible citizen

who was determined that his nephews, still in grammar school, should have a taste of competitive baseball. The year was 1938 and a total of three dozen kids got involved. Today, it is a far-reaching international product, covering thirty-one countries, nearly nine thousand leagues and two million children.

That Williamsport, Pennsylvania, should be the birthplace of this new religion amuses some who are unfamiliar with the chemistry of sport. Williamsport was once famous as a lumber town, one of those places where people put on a new mackintosh when they dressed up and parents read out loud to their sons from the works of Jack London. Why Williamsport? Why indeed. Why Shelby, Montana, for the Dempsey-Gibbons fight? Why Green Bay for the Packers? Why Sarajevo for the start of World War I?

The catalyst for all this was an unlikely fellow named Carl Stotz, an office worker for a Williamsport soft drink bottler. It would be nice to say that Carl Stotz had a dream, a vision. It would also be an embroidery of what is basically a classic story of American persistence. Large ideas are often born of small frustrations.

Stotz grew up loving baseball, mostly from a distance. The sandlot leagues in Williamsport—composed of Sunday school and company teams—were filled by the older fellows, who seemed to hold their positions in perpetuity. He was limited to games of workup in the park, that ageless pastime where an odd number of fellows got together, and when the hitter made an out he moved into the field and the fielders moved up one position, until each had a turn at bat. (Glorious fun, but you wouldn't want to make a career of it.)

Carl Stotz went through life's phases: school, job, marriage, a daughter. As a grown man he qualified for a few seasons in the local amateur leagues. Then, in the summer of 1938, when Carl was twenty-eight, his two nephews—Jimmy and Major Gehron, aged six and eight— came down with his old childhood malady: an incurable urge to play baseball. Carl decided that, by the beard of Abner Doubleday, there ought to be a place where his nephews and other neighborhood kids could not only enjoy a bat and a ball and their own imaginations, but get a sense of the game, the excitement, the sounds of human voices tuned to the action. He thought it would be fun to organize. Let them do on a grassy field what Carl Stotz had only done in his wildest daydreams. The American Legion and other teen leagues provided for the older boys. What was required, he concluded, was a league for the little guys. A little league.

Carl began to canvass the merchants of Williamsport, seeking funds to form his league and outfit the players. The first fifty-six people he approached refused. Some thought he was dotty. Others' laughed at the notion of little kids trying to play *hardball,* kids barely old enough to make a fist.

But Stotz persisted. Finally, a dairyman named Floyd Mutchler contributed $35, which Carl used to buy three dozen baseball-style playsuits at the local dime store to serve as uniforms for the teams. Next, smaller donations came from the Lundy Lumber Company and the Jumbo Pretzel Company, which paid for shirt emblems and some basic playing-field equipment. The Little League was in business.

Carl had put it together in time for the 1939 season. It amounted, that original year, to hardly more than supervised sandlot play. Such refinements as fences, scoreboards, dugouts and bleachers and other trappings existed only in the imagination of Carl Stotz and the kids who played—which meant that they existed nevertheless. Games were scheduled at twilight—as most still are—to allow the managers and adult supervisors time to beat it home from work, and early enough to get the kids in bed by a respectable hour. The men would bolt their suppers and hustle out to the vacant lot, their cars loaded with the essential equipment: home plate, a pitching slab, bases, bats and balls.

But in that first year, crude as the arrangements may have been, the basic principles were worked out. The age limit was set at twelve, on the theory that if they admitted thirteen- and fourteen-year-olds the smaller lads would be squeezed out. To determine the proper dimensions of the field, they staged lengthy tests of how far the little fellows could hit and throw effectively, and timed them at running bases. They finally settled on a diamond two-thirds the standard size, with 60 feet between bases and the pitcher standing 40 feet, 4 inches from home plate.

The number of innings a pitcher could work per week was strictly limited, and the length of a game was set at six innings. Playing rules were the same as in organized baseball, except that the runners could not leave their bases until the pitch reached the plate, and batters could not try for first on a dropped third strike.

With few adjustments, it is the same today as when the nephews of Carl Stotz suited up in 1939. The most significant change has seen the pitcher's mound moved back to 46 feet, reflecting the fact that America's young were getting bigger each year. With better nutrition and more affluence, they were adding pounds and inches.

The game of mini-baseball caught on instantly. The neighborhood grownups turned out by the hundreds to watch the three Williamsport teams compete. At the end of the season, official recognition arrived. The president of the Eastern League, Tommy Richardson, whose circuit was famed as a testing ground for future big league stars, promoted a public banquet honoring the kids. The movement—called Little League—was on its way.

The next year Carl Stotz had no problem attracting enough sponsors to finance a four-team league. They moved to a better playing area, on which the men had to first clear two hundred trees. In 1942 their field became the site of a war factory, and the momentum slowed. The world had plunged into war a few months before, and their fathers and older brothers were going off to fight it.

When the global tempers subsided, teams began to spring up around Williamsport like crabgrass. The idea soon spread around the state, and by 1947 it had infiltrated most of Pennsylvania, New York and New Jersey. All Star teams from those states met that year in a "national" tournament.

By 1948 Stotz and his friends were aware that they had been overtaken by events. The program—it was no longer thought of as a mere activity—had grown too large to be handled on a spare-time basis, and through tin cup donations. Stotz decided that a major new resource was needed. He went big game—big business—hunting. And he bagged his trophy.

It developed that United States Rubber Company was already interested in producing a special line of baseball sneakers for the small fry market. The upshot was that U.S. Rubber agreed to back an expanded national tournament in 1948. The company paid the traveling expenses of the teams, put them up at Williamsport's leading hotel and awarded prizes—gold medals and statuettes to every boy on the winning team, silver medals to the runners-up and bronze to the third place finishers. Lock Haven, Pennsylvania, won that mini-World Series—the first to gain national attention—by 6-5 over St. Petersburg, Florida.

From there kid baseball was to leap in size and influence, blanketing America, crossing the oceans, turning that $35 donation into a multi-million dollar industry. And, yet, for all its commercial overtones, and for all of its inherent *cuteness,* Little League is still faithful to the basic element that assured its success.

As Branch Rickey put it: "Baseball is a romance that begins when a boy is very young; it brings a diamond into his vision where the bases are fixed and the outfield is endless."

PART I

PART I

1. Hitting

The Most Difficult Job in Sports, but the Most Fun

When Theodore Samuel Williams was a teenager in San Diego, he drove his friends batty—no pun intended—by his insistence on practicing his hitting four hours a day, every day.

There always seemed to be a question of what Williams would run out of first: friends or daylight hours.

But that kind of dedication was to become the trademark of a fellow many consider the greatest lefthanded hitter of his time. As much as anyone who ever played the game, Ted Williams lived for his next time at bat. And what splendid times they were: six batting titles, two triple crowns, the MVP award twice, a lifetime average of .344. He was the last big leaguer to hit .400. At the mellow age of 42 he was *still* hitting over .300. He retired that season, 1960, with a home run in his last trip to the plate. They gave him the Comeback of the Year award.

No trophies were needed to establish the fact that T.S. Williams was special. In a time when most players seemed to be stamped out of punch presses, Ted stood apart, custom made, one of a kind. He disliked the circus that always follows fame. His life existed between the white lines of the field. He didn't even go to movies for fear of tiring his eyes.

Of his natural assets, the vision of Ted Williams most accounted for his consistency as a hitter. With gunscope eyes, he missed nothing. He had the uncanny ability to follow the ball to the instant it collided with his bat.

Williams' eyesight, on or off the field, was legendary. Joe Reichler, later with the baseball commissioner's office but then with the Associated Press, tells of a time that Ted was lolling on the beach in Florida one spring, talking with reporters. Suddenly, he looked far down the sands and exclaimed, "Wow, get a load of that!"

"I looked down the beach," said Reichler, "and I saw this nice shape in a skimpy suit. I could just about make her out."

"Some body," added Williams, "but she has too much hair on her legs."

"WE'LL GET THIS DOUBLEHEADER OVER WITH IN NO TIME."

Not everyone is born with super-perfect vision, of course, and few can develop the dedication of a Ted Williams. But the hard work, practice, the constant striving for improvement that Williams represented—there lies the road to greatness, fellow ball players.

Surprisingly, from one who was famous for his own volatile temper, Ted insists that what you will need most of is patience. "It looks easy," he says, "but baseball is the hardest game to play. This game needles you. You get a pitch you should have hit and you have to wait three innings to get another shot. In football you make a mistake, or you're frustrated, and you can knock the hell out of somebody and say, 'Take that you (expletive deleted)'."

In the years between his career as a player and his return to the majors as a manager (in Washington, D.C., and Texas), Williams often lectured at baseball clinics. He was in his element on those occasions, talking about a science that excited him, explaining, asking questions, urging the kids to hit for themselves, not for Ted Williams.

In Ted's gospel, rules are second to style. Get the feeling, the groove, the easy ride that tells you, yes, this is your best way. Most of the great ones make the same point. "I'd try to help a young player with his own style," says Hank Aaron, who broke Ruth's record, "not mine."

What Ted Williams says about hitting, you can take as truth. Just remember, if the ball doesn't always explode off the bat as it did from his, there is *plenty* of room for hitters below Ted Williams.

These, then, are the essentials of Ted's tips to the young ball player:

The bat. The weight of the bat is most important. When a boy or girl picks up a bat and says, "Hey, this feels good," then the weight is right—not too heavy. Picking a bat is like trying on a coat: You *know* if it fits. Heft it, balance it, decide if it feels light enough and long enough. A lot of young fellows like to know how to hold a bat. Williams once asked this same question of a great hitter—Ty Cobb—about twenty-five years ago and this is what he said: "Pick up the bat like an axe and form a simple V off the handle. Put your hands up to your shoulders. As you settle in at the plate, you will find yourself moving your hands around to a comfortable position." From there, it's pretty much an individual feel.

The strike zone. Certainly, one of the most important things youngsters have to learn is the importance of the strike zone, which means the width of the plate, above the knees and slightly under the armpits. Now, the more critical you are in assessing the strike zone, the easier it will be for you to develop into a good hitter, for you'll be ahead of the pitcher more often. In other words, instead of having to swing at marginal pitches, two or three inches off the edge of the plate, because the count is against you, you'll have him in the hole. When you swing at questionable pitches you *increase* the strike zone for the pitcher, and you'll be getting fewer good balls to hit.

Hands and wrists. One of the most important phases of hitting is being quick with your hands and wrists. This will really determine just how good a hitter you're going to be. The faster you snap those wrists, the longer you can wait for the pitch, and the less likely you are to be fooled. To strengthen your hands and wrists, practice push-ups, chin-ups and squeezing a rubber ball. The best exercise of all is to get a bat that weighs 8 or 10 ounces more than the one you use in a game and just keep swinging it. Keep swinging it. Imagine a pitch as you look toward an imaginary pitcher. Pretend the pitch is low and outside. Be quick with the swing. . . *and keep swinging.* Here's how to do it, point by point: (1) Imagine the pitch being delivered; (2) as you stride, your hands fall back slightly; (3) as you anticipate you're going to swing, your hips start moving; (4) as your hips start opening up, your hands follow through; (5) as you hit the ball, your wrists haven't broken yet, but as you contact the ball your wrists start breaking; *not before,* just at the point of impact and as you follow through.

"YOU'RE CHOKING THE BAT TOO MUCH, SIMMS."

Bad habits. The problem a lot of young hitters have is trying to eliminate a hitch. What is a hitch? It's simply dropping the hands as you anticipate going in towards the pitch; dropping your hands and then coming up to the plate where you're going to hit the ball. A hitch is harmful because it takes time to drop your hands. It takes time to move up and the thing you're trying to do is be quick with your hands and wrists. A hitch takes enough time that you have to commit yourself sooner about going into the pitch. It is much better if you can keep your hands steady and still, without dropping them sharply.

The stride. Another question often asked is how far should a young hitter stride. Avoid taking an extremely closed stance—that is, keeping your feet together—and making a long stride. This causes your head to move and takes up more time. A slightly spread stance enables you to use a shorter stride, jerks your head less and gets you to the ball faster. Also, your eyes are given a clearer look at the ball.

Balance. You're in the batter's box, relaxed, ready, in the right position to stride and swing. Everything should be in balance. The weight should be toward the front of the foot, on the balls of the feet, *never* on the heels, because this will rob you of power. Keep the weight evenly distributed on both feet while in the ready position.

Where to stand. In most kid baseball leagues, you needn't worry about the big curve. A lot of fellows prefer to dig in at the extreme rear of the batter's box, on the theory that this allows you more time to look at the pitch. This is all right if you're not expecting a curve. But for those times when the competition is faster, remember, the further away the hitter is from the plate, the bigger the break he has to handle. Crowd the plate if you have to, but line up even with it. By being even, you only have to cover pitches right over the plate, right where you can hit 'em.

TRIM

IIow to break a slump. The easiest way to fall into a slump is by trying to pull the ball too much. Pulling is the hardest way to hit. To pull the ball you have to swing sooner, commit yourself sooner and even anticipate the pitch. The pitcher, of course, is trying to keep the hitter off balance. The answer is to just get the bat on the ball, and don't worry about trying to knock down fences. Choke up a bit—grab the bat a bit farther from the handle—and shorten your swing. By choking up on the bat you'll have a better chance of hitting it consistently through the middle. Turn toward the pitcher with your front shoulder down and in. Step toward the mound so that your momentum and weight are directed back at the pitcher. This helps you do one essential thing: keep your head down. You're looking at the pitch all the time. When you commit yourself too soon your head tends to flop like a rag doll, and you're going to get fooled.

Hitting is the single most difficult task in sports. A computer couldn't keep track of all the things that go into it. And every day you see something new.

Summing up:

1. Use the right bat for you, one you can handle comfortably.

2. Use a grip that's firm, but not so tight as to lock your wrists.

3. Wait for a good pitch to hit, one that is in the strike zone.

4. Work at being quick with your hands and wrists: the quicker you become, the longer you can wait to judge the pitch.

5. Eliminate or minimize any lost motion so you can gain time.

6. Use a short, quick stride because it is faster, your head moves less and you can see the pitch better.

7. Be in balance at all times while in the batter's box.

8. Stand close to and even with the plate so you can cover it more easily and hit with more authority.

9. The more you practice, the better a hitter you will become.

10. Get the bat on the ball. Don't worry about trying to hit it out of the park.

2. Pitching and Catching

David Clyde and Johnny Bench Tell How They Began

David Clyde, the baby southpaw of the Texas Rangers, has little difficulty remembering how it was when he started kid baseball—it hasn't been that long since he was there. When Clyde first came to the Rangers in 1973, fresh out of high school at age eighteen and the Number One pick of all the baseball draft, the novelty of his great jump drew a capacity 33,000 crowd to the Texas ballpark.

Organized baseball can almost count on the fingers of one hand the players who went immediately to the Big League and never played anywhere else. The legendary Mel Ott, out of Gretna, Louisiana, was one. Joe Nuxhall pitched for Cincinnati when he was fifteen, and fireballing Lew Krausse was a celebrated bonus baby at Kansas City. But both Nuxhall and Krausse later had to put in time in the minor leagues before cementing a career at the top level. When Clyde put on a major league uniform and indicated he would never wear any other kind, historians traced all the way back to Bob Feller in the 1930s, coming out of high school in Van Meter, Iowa, to find another such young talent.

Clyde's views on pitching, and his advice for youngsters

starting out are still one and the same. "It's my ambition to be a control pitcher, not a strikeout pitcher," he says, "And that's what a young pitcher should work on, first, last and forever. Control. Throwing strikes. There is one main way to do this, and that's practice, practice, practice. There's no other way. You have to throw every day, and every pitch you throw you have to be concentrating on throwing a strike. When I was eleven I was wild as a March hare. I'd walk the bases loaded and then strike out the side. I've always been able to throw hard, but to win you have to get the ball over the plate."

Clyde was helped all along in his development by the expert advice, encouragement and active participation of his father, Eugene, who still coaches kid baseball in Houston. The elder Clyde gave his son invaluable tips on correcting control problems:

The line of lime toward the plate. "If you draw a line right down the middle of the mound," says David Clyde, "toward home plate, you want to have your lead foot come down either right on the line or a little to the off-side. In my case, being a lefthander, I'd want my right foot to come down on the line or to the third base side of the line. A righthander should have his foot on the line or to the first base side. This does two things—it lines up your motion with your target, home plate, and it prevents you from throwing across your body. When you throw across your body, you're not getting all your body into the pitch and you're putting unnatural strain on your arm."

Clyde's father recommends making the imaginary line an actual fact by using a bit of the lime that marks the batting box and the foul lines.

Eugene Clyde also insisted that David come straight overhead with his throwing motion, because that is ideal. It delivers more power with less strain on the arm. Both father and son agree, however, that if the overhand style is "uncomfortable" for a youngster, and he can throw strikes more often with a three-quarter motion, or even sidearm, then he should do so. Another of the Clyde sons threw "submarine" style.

"More important than any fundamentals," says Eugene Clyde, "is for the boy to realize his own limitations; to set a standard for himself which he thinks he can reach. That's all I ever ask any kid to do. That is, perform as good as he's capable of performing. That way baseball is fun, which is what it's meant to be."

The fundamentals of control, in addition to daily throwing, are fairly simple. *Wild high*: This results from either not striding forward far enough with the lead foot or releasing the ball too soon in the delivery. *Wild low*: The exact opposite; the stride is too far or the release is too late. By concentrating on the most common error of wildness, the basic flow in the pitching motion can be corrected.

Use the pitcher's mound. It may never occur to young pitchers why the mound is built up higher than home plate, and what advantage there is in having the ledge of the "rubber" to help the body's motion in delivering the ball. A righthander should practice using leverage of the right foot braced against the rubber (or an anchored plank board in his back yard) to get the thrust of his whole body behind the velocity of the pitch. Flex the knees and *drive* off the rubber.

The wind-up. Using the rubber for leverage, a young pitcher will naturally evolve his own style of starting the pitching motion and following through. This should be basic and elemental at first, beginning with both hands at the waist, left foot slightly back of the right foot (for a righthander)—just slightly different from an ordinary game of "catch." Bit by bit the young pitcher will advance into a style that fits his own physique and arm angle. An artificial copying of some favorite big leaguer as seen on TV could set a youngster off in the wrong direction.

"I WASN'T SWINGING LATE...HE WAS PITCHING EARLY."

The "other" pitch. Five out of seven pitches by a young pitcher should be the fast ball. But he does need "something else" to keep batters from eventually getting their timing coordinated with his delivery. In no case should this something else be the curve ball. "I never threw a curve ball growing up," says David Clyde. "A kid's bones are not developed enough to stand the strain of throwing a curve." What Clyde used was a "slip pitch" (his own term). The effect was to give the batter a different pitch to look at when he is expecting a fast ball.

"I made a 'C' of my thumb and first finger," Clyde says, "and placed the baseball as far back in the 'C' as I could. I put my second finger right alongside my first finger and then I threw it with the same motion as my fast ball, letting it slip out. The batters actually thought it was a curve."

Clyde's dad began working with him at age six, and at age seven the youngster was playing in a junior league. "It worked out for my boy," the elder Clyde says, "but I certainly don't recommend it for others. I think age eleven is the soonest that a youngster should be put in a competitive level, one where you try out for a team and get cut."

The correct grip. When youngsters begin throwing a baseball at age eight or nine, their hands simply are not big enough to hold it properly. They compensate by using all of their fingers in holding and throwing the ball. By age eleven or twelve most are capable of using the right grip, the one that will afford a better result from wrist-snap in delivery. The baseball should be gripped as nearly at the end of the first two fingers as possible with the thumb underneath and the last two fingers tucked down. The top fingers should grip the ball across the long seams, with the first two joints getting good traction against the front seam.

The palm ball. This is an ideal alternative pitch to the

aforementioned slip pitch as a change-of-speed delivery to make the fast ball that much more effective. It is one that Eugene Clyde taught David and still teaches to other young pitchers today. The baseball is shoved back against the palm, gripped with all the fingers, and thrown with a "stiff wrist"–that is, without the usual downward snap of the wrist in throwing a fastball. The arm motion is the same as the fast ball, but the ball will arrive at the plate in a much different fashion than the standard pitch.

"Above all," says David Clyde, "you have got to practice a lot or all the rest of it doesn't mean a thing. If you can't throw strikes, they'll get somebody in there who can. A fellow's best friend is the one who will catch for him when he needs the work."

And speaking of a pitcher's best friend–the Committee for Fairness to Catchers ought to do something about that scurrilous phrase, "the tools of ignorance," which in certain insensitive circles is used to describe the catcher's armor.

Of course, one of the things that makes it so hard to overcome this unfortunate image is the fact that the phrase was turned by one of their own–yes, a catcher, Muddy Ruel, then with the Washington Senators, where his job was to receive the legendary fast balls of Walter Johnson.

On further study, it is possible to offer a deeper meaning to Muddy's immortal line. If catchers need to be ignorant of *anything* it is pain and fatigue. Let's be honest. It is not exactly a gentle position. No one enjoys those noisy collisions at the plate, or getting hit with foul tips or wild pitches. But some tolerate them better than others.

One who does is Johnny Bench, of the Cincinnati Reds, who has become the modern prototype of what the complete catcher should be. "The first requirement for a kid catcher," says Bench, "is to overcome the fear of getting hit by the ball. A young kid will get bruised. It takes some durability and a lot of patience and understanding of the fact that you are going to get hurt at various times. You just have to accept it as part of the game."

The story of Johnny Bench will serve as a beacon for all the young catchers of tomorrow. He was born in Oklahoma City on the anniversary of Pearl Harbor, December 7, 1947. He was raised down the road at Binger, Okla., a town with a population of 730, which Johnny describes as lying "two miles beyond Resume Speed."

Detecting signs of an early talent in his son, Ted Bench created an organized team in Binger for Johnny and his two older brothers. Papa Bench encouraged Johnny to catch, on the theory—a good one—that it was the quickest path to the big leagues. He played other positions at times, and as a pitcher even fashioned a 16-1 record his sophomore year in high school. But in his own mind, and those of the scouts who were soon trailing him, Johnny Bench was a catcher. "Maybe," he concedes, "it was because I hit .675 in high school."

There is something about the position, of course, that inspires fierce loyalty among those who play it. The catcher winds up with the dirtiest uniform. He suffers more physical demands. And, most prideful of all, he is *in* the game, every blessed pitch of it.

It isn't enough that he is able to catch or hit, he must act as a kind of manager on the field, which may indicate why so many former catchers wind up running their own teams—Mickey Cochrane, Ralph Houk, Yogi Berra, Del Crandall, Paul Richards and countless others. He must use his brains and at times a touch of psychology. Once, when Bench felt his pitcher was not throwing with as much force as he could, he shocked the whole ball park by arrogantly catching a pitch with his bare hand. The pitcher got the point, and proceeded to bear down.

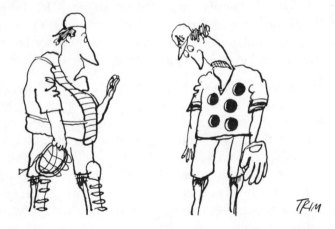

"SETTLE DOWN ... THEY'RE STARTING TO HIT YOU PRETTY HARD."

Bench has trained himself to catch the ball with one hand, and to cock and fire from a crouch, two techniques now widely used in the major leagues. As a youngster, he practiced for hour upon hour, transferring the ball swiftly from glove to throwing hand while still in his crouch, always making sure that he grasped the ball exactly across the seams so that his pegs to second and third never curved or tailed. In time it became automatic.

He has what is known in the baseball idiom as "soft hands," meaning that he gathers in the pitch, he doesn't fight it. For a catcher, part of this is a natural gift, the rest will come with experience. It is done in much the same way as a receiver in football draws in a pass.

Few catchers have experienced the golden moments of Johnny Bench. Since he broke in with the Reds in 1968, he has won Rookie of the Year and Most Valuable Player awards; he has played in a winning World Series; became the first catcher in history to lead either major league in homers. All of which is even more remarkable when you consider that the rigors of the job are expected to reduce a catcher's effectiveness at bat. For one thing, squatting is not a natural position. It tends to tighten the leg muscles, the main reason that catchers as base runners are often the subject of dugout humor. Thus, the catcher who can hit, and run, increases his value to the team.

For more "inside" on catching, here's Johnny Bench:

Equipment. "I remember, when I was a kid, that the awkwardness of the catching gear took some getting used to. I learned early that it was important to get the right equipment, which meant the glove and the mask and the chest protector and shin guards. It's important that they fit. If they fit properly, you improve your mobility and cut down on the chance of being injured."

Handling the pitch. One-handed catching has now become the most common style. "I not only recommend it to kids," says Bench, "I recommend it to everybody. First of all, it lessens the chance of injury. Second, it puts you in a quicker position to throw. The trick is to get the right kind of glove, one that reacts like a first baseman's glove, one that is flexible."

Developing your arm. "The best advice I ever got as a youngster," says Johnny, "was to learn to throw by my ear, and to take pride in my arm. Try to protect it. Warm up slowly." A young catcher can build up his arm by throwing distances far in excess of home plate to second base. Long distance throwing will increase the muscles in your arm and strengthen them. Bench doesn't recommend lifting weights.

Pop flies. The key thing is to wait for the ball to reach its maximum height, the apex, then go *after* the ball (unless it's a long way off and you must break with the ball). Of course, you must get the mask off almost by instinct, and remember to throw it in the direction opposite that from which you'll be running, so you don't trip over it. The catcher must know his own abilities, whether or not he can make a certain play. If he thinks he can make it he must take charge. If he sees he can't, he has to make the call for the infielder or pitcher who can.

Blocking the plate. Never, repeat never, block the plate without the ball. Unless you have the ball you're just asking to get run over, which is a quick way to get hurt. Protect your legs by keeping the toe pointed at the runner, rather than to the side. If you get hit from the side you may jerk that knee, which leads to the kind of injury that can shorten your career.

Summary. Avoid injury by: (1) using only one hand, (2) staying away from blocking home plate when it is unnecessary, (3) wearing the right equipment, and (4) taking care of your body. You can give the pitcher confidence, and win his in you, by achieving consistency behind the plate—doing your job every day.

Okay, catchers. There it is. Wear your tools well, and with pride. They stand for endurance and persistence, not ignorance, after all.

STRIKE ONE, TWO AND THREE ! "

3. The Infield

The Best Athletes Belong Here

One of the truly great advances in fatherhood, it is worth remembering, was inspired by the baseball infield. This was in the days when daddy was taught to diaper a baby by folding home plate to second base, and pinning first and third to the pitcher's mound. Or something like that.

We recall this now by way of stressing the importance of the corners of infield play. The boys in the middle—short and second—may handle more ground balls, but the pressure points are and always will be first and third.

Accordingly, the guest lecturers in this chapter are Willie McCovey, San Diego's slugging first baseman, and Doug Rader, Houston's colorful third sacker. The advice of McCovey and Rader can benefit the emerging young player not just because of their talent and experience and attitudes, but because both remember what it was like to be a kid, learning not to flinch. Rader puts it aptly, drawing on his own childhood experiences in Northbrook, Illinois:

"I think instruction, and the emphasis, in kid baseball is often in the wrong place. The most important thing is for them to *play*. Kids today are overinstructed. The more they play the better they will be able to judge which advice to follow.

"When I was a kid my dad, and a few of the other dads, maybe four or five of them, helped out with our neighborhood team. We had a little park across the road from a tavern. They'd dump all the equipment and say, 'Okay, you boys get together and choose up teams and play.' Then they'd go across the street and have a couple of beers, and let us play. Every hour or so my dad would stick his head out the door and walk to the edge of the road and rub his hand across his shirt a few times—you know, flashing me the hit-and-run sign, or something. That's how we practiced. It was different for the games, of course, but we learned by participating. The kid who has the ability, the desire, if he plays it will surface. You can't force it."

Willie McCovey has been one of baseball's legendary power hitters for a dozen years. But he is so worth hearing because of the things he could not do, the weaknesses he had to overcome. At one stage of his career he was booed and jeered by the home fans. His own abundant pride won them over.

Willie never complained when the San Francisco Giants shuttled him between first base and the outfield, trying to find a lineup that could include both his bat and Orlando Cepeda's. His experience in left field came from on-the-job training, and for a young, gangling specimen like McCovey (6-4 and then 195) it led to uneasy times. One day, back at first base, he dropped a pop fly and the crowd laughed out loud.

In the same game, the Giants' third baseman, Harvey Kuenn, also dropped one, and the crowd reacted not at all. This puzzled Alvin Dark, then the San Francisco manager. "Why is it funny when McCovey loses a pop-up," he asked a writer, later, "and not funny when Kuenn does it?"

"Well, for one thing," answered the writer, "McCovey's hit him on the head."

"It did not," snapped Dark. "It hit him on the bill of his cap."

It is a measure of Willie McCovey's resolution that by the end of the decade he would be accepted as a master of his position. He acquired his own special rooting section in Candlestick Park, an anthill of small kids who would congregate behind the wire fence in right field, waiting for Willie to swat one.

There is one quality the young first baseman must have, says McCovey, and it can't be practiced. Pride. He is tired of reading about first base as though it were a refuge for those who are so uncoordinated they can't sing and take a shower at the same time. "It's a key position," he says, "because you're involved in so many plays, and you get all kinds of throws. Contrary to what a lot of guys think, it isn't some kind of rest home where you stick the people who can't play anywhere else, or who have come to the end of their career. That's not true at all. You can ask Willie Mays and Hank Aaron about that."

No one has ever accused third base of being a rest home. In the mid-seventies no one was playing the position better than Doug Rader, acclaimed by many as the successor to Brooks Robinson as baseball's most complete hot corner man. Doug brought something else to the job, a sense of proportion. Once, interviewed on television, he suggested that youngsters just learning the game should eat bubble gum cards. Not the bubble gum, mind you, but the cards, "which have lots of information on them about hitting and pitching."

Doug Rader belongs in a category with Pete Rose of the Reds, fellows who fight and hustle and are willing to take a fast ball on the elbow if it will win a game. Rader has a pixie quality, as well; he is turned on by the pure joy of being a ball player. He is a fine example for any beginner.

"Kid baseball," he says now, "was a very pleasurable experience for me. Relaxed. The parents would come out and have a picnic in the stands and talk about the PTA and let the kids play. And that was fun. It was low-keyed and good times."

We have compressed and organized the thoughts of McCovey and Rader as they apply to general infield play. You will find slightly more detail on their positions because the plays at the corners are more testing and varied.

FIRST BASE: "You must have good hands and a long reach," says McCovey. "I'd advise most of you shorties to go find another position." One needn't be a ballet dancer, but you must be agile enough to handle the different throws coming at you from all around the infield, including pickoff plays by the pitcher, and the hard snap throw by a second baseman charging a slow roller. That one can handcuff you. Try to reach out and get every ball before it hits the dirt. Now that isn't always possible, obviously, but anytime you can go out and meet it you'll have a better chance of saving the throw.

Playing the bag. Where he positions himself depends upon what kind of hitter is at bat. This is why the other team should be observed in batting practice. Since few youngsters are quick enough with the bat to pull the ball, the usual rules don't apply (such as shifting toward the line for a lefty hitter). The important point is for the first baseman *not* to get so far from the bag that he can't get there before the runner.

Taking the throw. Straddle the bag until the ball is hit. This provides a better target and a better chance to maneuver if the throw is off. The first baseman should not try to shift his feet on the wide side as big leaguers do. He should tag the bag always with the same foot, the one opposite his gloved hand. It may not look as slick, but will cut down on errors. And even the big boys have trouble with their footwork. When the Giants moved Willie Mays to first base, he had a problem shifting. But after you work at it a while, finding the bag with your foot becomes automatic.

Fielding the bunt. You have to make an instant judgment on what kind of bunt is coming, and that will determine whether to charge or stay back. If the bunt is away from you, it is better for the first baseman to get back and take the throw, rather than let the second baseman cover. If it's a close play, the reach and experience of the first baseman could make the difference.

The double play. Probably *the* toughest play for a first baseman to make is the 3-6-3 (first-to-short-to-first) double play. It will be extremely rare in most kid baseball leagues—where any double play is rare—but it is worth practicing because it will sharpen his timing. The first baseman must field the ball, make a perfect throw to the shortstop—that is, put the ball where he wants it, and no two want it in the same spot—then get back to first, find the bag with his foot and take the throw coming back. All of that happens in a matter of a few seconds.

Leadership. The first baseman has to be willing to be involved. If the pitcher is struggling, he's right there, in a good position to encourage him and try to settle him down. Also, he should be alert to signals from the bench. The manager might want him to go out to the mound and stall a bit, while a relief pitcher warms up. Whatever the situation, the team has to have a feeling of security about the guy at first base. Ninety percent of the time, says Willie McCovey, they can't complete a play without him.

SHORTSTOP AND SECOND BASE: There are a few general rules that apply to all infielders. To begin with, always know what the situation is: how many are out, how many on, what base the play will be depending on where the ball is hit. Says Doug Rader: "I can have a ball hit to me the same way five or six nights in a row, and the play is different each time because of the situation. . . depending on the outs and the runners. It comes with experience, but the young player has to ask, or be reminded, until it is second nature, where to go if a ball gets through the infield or is hit down the line; who to back up, who the cutoff men are, who the relay men are. All of it is crucial."

Rader goes on: "The fun is in being able to handle the ball. Mastering that part of it. Gaining that confidence. A lot of kids hope that the ball *isn't* hit to them. That's not good. You shouldn't be afraid of making an error. You're going to make some. But the more aggressive you are, the more you *want* the ball hit to you, the less chance there is of making a mistake. The idea is to reach a point where you feel disappointed any time the ball isn't hit at you."

Grounders. The first thing the infielder must learn is that there is a right way to go down for a ground ball. The good fielder doesn't bend from the waist. He bends from the knees. The feet should be slightly farther apart than the shoulders. "Start on a square foundation," suggests Rader. "The big thing is to be in a position to break one way or another. You can't just stand flatfooted and expect to be able to react. You have to come up on your toes and get a little rhythm going with your body, a kind of rocking chair motion, as the pitch is coming, so you can break quickly. That's where a lot of kids make a mistake. They shorten up one way, or get a foot too far in front of the other. Consequently, I would start squared, and take two little shovel steps and come up on my toes."

Using the glove. Keep the glove directly in front of and under the ground ball. The more of the glove's surface you expose to the path of the ball, the better your chance of stopping it. And the first objective is to *stop* the ball, even if it isn't handled cleanly. Kids will be playing on fields that are rough, getting bounces that are not true. And stopping the ball, keeping it from going through the infield, frequently means the difference between one base and several in kid leagues. Beginners should be taught to watch the ball into their glove. This is the best way to condition them not to jerk their heads when they reach down to field the ball. The youngster will overcome his fear of a batted ball when he has fielded enough of them to know that he can handle them.

Double plays. Rare as they may be, the double play is well worth working for because nothing exhilarates a team more, or demoralizes an opponent faster. If you are the relay man, you are the key. You must catch the throw, tag second, get out of the way of the runner, then throw hard and accurately to first. You should tag second and cross it. *Never* stand there. You become a target for the runner coming in, who will take you out if he can. That's his job. But it's also up to the runner to get out of the way of the ball. So make your throw to first as though he weren't there. Make it head high. This will have the effect of making him start his slide earlier, and give you an edge in getting out of the way.

As middle men in the dp, the shortstop crosses the bag with his left foot and takes one step with his right to make the throw; the second baseman puts his left foot on the bag, takes one step to plant his right and then throws to first. But he should always remember: the main concern is to get the out at second, then try for the double play if he can. When in doubt, *hold* the throw to first. Don't risk throwing the ball away. The key to the double play is to concentrate on one step at a time.

For coaches, here's a useful drill to help the boys and girls get their teamwork down. Sit behind the mound and roll fifty balls to the second baseman, and fifty to the shortstop, with each starting the double play in motion. Once a week will be enough.

Force plays. Assign one player to cover second when the runner on first is moving, either on a grounder or if the ball gets away from the catcher. In the pros, who covers depends on how the hitter bats. There is no need to get that sophisticated at the kid baseball level. Just be sure the player assigned knows his job.

Tagging the runner. The best way to do this is to straddle the bag, catch the ball with two hands and, with the bare hand over the glove, drop the hands down in front of the bag. Let the runner slide into the tag. Even if he is safe keep the ball on him until the play has ended. He might overslide or take his foot off base, as often happens in a game of kid baseball.

Pop flies. Back pedaling is absolutely ruled out. The infielder should turn and run sideways, trying to get around and in back of the ball, if he can, or catching it on the run, if he must. On all pop flies hit out of the infield, the centerfielder is the quarterback, the one who will "call" which player should catch it, unless the ball is down the line. Then the nearest outfielder should call it. The reason for this is simple. The outfielder is coming in, and has a clearer view of the play than the turning, twisting infielder.

How and when to throw. A three-quarter arm motion will be the most natural for the young infielder, especially on those plays where there is no time to "wind up." The second baseman must also be able to get off the quick snap peg, underhanded, when moving toward the first baseman. This has to be a "controlled" throw, sharp but not overpowering, to avoid tearing his head off. The first baseman has a tough throw of his own, to the pitcher covering the bag. He must judge the pitcher's speed and keep the throw chest high, so he won't have to bend over while he's running. And it should be in front of him, so he doesn't have to reach back.

Always get set when you can, but be prepared to come up throwing. Make sure the ball is cleanly gripped before throwing it. The infielder should play it safe and *not* throw, when the play at first seems doubtful. As the season wears on, his ability to judge the speed of the batted ball and the speed of the runner will improve, and will tell him when he has time and when he doesn't.

The bunt. This is baseball's version of the fire drill. Every player has his station. In the basic bunt situation—man on first, one out or none—the first and third basemen will move toward the batter; the second baseman will cover the first and the shortstop moves to second base. If the pitcher isn't in a position to field the ball, he should be alert to back up either first or third, in the event of a wild throw. Once contact with the ball is made, and it is clear which fielder will take the ball, the nearest teammate can use his lungs to guide the play. He can do this by yelling out whether a force is possible at second, or to go for the out at first base. Often, the pitcher is in the best position to do this. There is one cardinal rule on the bunt: everybody must be somewhere. It is unforgivable to be standing around, between bases, even if someone else is making the play. This is one of those moments when the player can anticipate the action. He can back up a base.

THIRD BASE: Doug Rader says: "To play here a kid has to be fairly aggressive. He has to be willing to get banged around a little, to play the hot drive, the one-hopper or the liner that bounces up and off his chest. His reflexes aren't developed yet. I can think back to when I was that age, you just weren't physically able to cope with the ball that was hit like a shot. But the youngster has one great thing going for him: he can develop quickness. All it is, is hand and eye coordination. To do this, to develop his quickness, he ought to play at normal depth, maybe even a little shallow. You don't want him playing back, trying to cover up a shortcoming, or he'll never get any better."

Playing the line. It depends on the range of the player, but in most cases he should play about 10 feet to the left of the bag. If he hugs the line he has to cut his range in half. Even in the majors, balls hit over the third base bag are rare. And in kid baseball, more often than not, *any* ball hit through the infield has a chance to go for extra bases.

The slow roller. This is the ball the third baseman must charge and, most of the time, throw on the run. If the runner has a good start, and any speed, it is a tough play to beat. As a rule of thumb, don't throw if the runner is already in your sight, directly between you and the first baseman. If there is a slight chance, however, aim the ball and cut loose. You won't know if the play can be made unless you risk it.

Conclusions: It is estimated that 85 percent of the players who sign pro contracts, not including pitchers, have played in the infield as youngsters. Mickey Mantle, Hank Aaron, Pete Rose, César Cedeno, among dozens of other recent and current outfield stars, began their careers as infielders. If this suggests anything, it is that Little Leaguers face no urgency in terms of where they play, if they lose their slowness to learn the game's more sophisticated techniques. The fun is in conquering the batted ball.

4. The Outfield

Unlocking the Mysteries of a Fly Ball

At its most exalted level, the outfield is the glamour position, the place where the superstars roam. Ty Cobb, Babe Ruth, Joe DiMaggio, Mickey Mantle, Hank Aaron, Reggie Jackson. Their names roll out like thunder. And the thunder is associated with the bat. Which is where young Jeff Burroughs comes in. The Texas Ranger rightfielder could be the next superhero of the home run. In any case, he is part of the new young breed who have come out of 1960s kid baseball to make bundles of money while playing for fun.

Burroughs' beginnings followed a classic pattern. "I played ball with the kids around the neighborhood," he says, "and then we played softball in grammar school, and we just naturally started playing baseball right after that." Burroughs played at age eight in an Elks league, and a year later began head-to-head competition with eleven- and twelve-year–olds in Little League, as a shortstop and pitcher.

That's the way it usually goes at the twelve-and-under level. The good athletes are put in the infield and the ones who can't handle a ground ball are "hidden" at various places in the outfield.

But it ain't necessarily so. If a particular youngster's reflexes aren't advanced enough at eleven or twelve to qualify for the infield, he can still be a highly valuable team member at one of the outfield positions—through practice. The mysteries of a fly ball dropping down out of the sky—the optical illusion, for instance, that at the last bit of the arc it is dropping *straight* down—all disappear after a kid has caught a thousand or two. Aside from the acquired skills that repetition produces, it also results in the most important asset to a young outfielder:

Confidence: "Any ballplayer has to believe in himself," says Burroughs, "believe he can get the job done. This is confidence. A talented ballplayer without confidence will

"HE'LL BE OKAY SOON AS HE GETS A LITTLE CONFIDENCE."

not do as good a job as a lesser ballplayer who thinks he can do it." This is Burroughs' baseball version of positive thinking, and the surest way to get hold of this quality is for the youngster to have someone hit, or throw, fly balls to him hour after hour.

Go all out. Burroughs doesn't believe the ten-to-twelve age is too young for a prospective athlete to begin finding out about himself. "Aside from all the fundamentals, if a kid has an idea he might want to be something someday in baseball, he should dedicate himself to running as fast as he can, throwing as hard as he can and hitting as hard as he can. He should test his limits. He may discover that he'll develop his muscles and his talents far beyond what another kid does who isn't putting all out every minute the way he is. This is the way Arnold Palmer and Jack Nicklaus got to be great golfers. They were told to hit it as hard as they could and never mind about the direction the ball went. Later on they could take care of the direction, but from the start they wanted the most important thing, putting everything they had into hitting the ball."

With that basic in mind, there are different roles for outfielders according to their positions in left, right and center:

Rightfield: This should be the proudest spot in the outfield, because more chances are directed here by the late-hitting batters. The rightfielder should have the best arm of the three outfielders, not only for the throw to the plate, but also for the difficult chore of throwing out a runner advancing from first to third on a ball hit past the infield.

Leftfield: The leftfielder has less to do than the other

players; in kid baseball, the ball is not often hit directly into the leftfield. But the leftfielder needs to practice on stopping ground balls that get through the infield. If he handles his position well, he can save extra base hits and runs.

Centerfield: Speed is the required ability here, for the centerfielder to cut off drives that are hit between him and his partners in left and right. The centerfielder also has the responsibility of being the quarterback on short fly balls, calling out who is to take the catch.

The three will share in the other fundamentals of outfield play:

Concentration: At any age an outfielder can be distracted and allow his mind to wander from the game, if he isn't *intent on what's happening. Therefore, he should move with every pitch.* That is, he should be up on the balls of his feet, leaning forward and beginning to take a step as the pitcher delivers the ball to the plate. This is how professional baseball stars "get the jump on the ball." It is also a great way to keep in tune with the game. Another part of concentration by an outfielder is knowing before the ball is pitched where he will throw if the ball is hit to him.

Charge the ground ball: Any ground ball that gets past the infield should be taken by the outfielder as close to the infield as he can rush to meet it.

Make sure the ball doesn't get through: Big innings when a high number of runs are scored usually decide these games, and it often falls to the outfielder to stop the base-clearing hit. Unless he has proven to be an exceptionally sure fielder, he should always drop to one knee when fielding a ground ball. This will guarantee that the ball won't get past him. On a bounding ball, of course, he must try to time his approach to take the ball on the high bounce and be in good throwing position.

The three greatest defensive outfielders in the game are generally acknowledged to be Tris Speaker, Joe DiMaggio and Terry Moore. (The last, while with the St. Louis Cardinals, never had the batting averages the other two recorded.) **1925155**

DiMaggio has some tips that are so elemental kid players can benefit by the advice: "The outfielder must try to make every catch in the best position to throw. I took fly balls with my hands above my head, with my left foot toward the plate, to save time making the throw. . . .

"On throws to all bases, including home plate, a throw on one hop is preferable to a throw on the fly. A bounding throw is more accurate and far easier for an infielder to handle, and bounce throws are far less likely to get away from the man making the catch. . . .

"Position yourself deep. The hardest thing for an outfielder to do is go back on a fly ball. *Backpedaling outfielders get nowhere on balls hit behind them.* If a ball is hit beyond you, the only thing to do is turn around and run and try to get behind it before it comes down.

"An outfielder should take an occasional infield workout to keep his eye sharp for ground balls."

Two faults are so common to young outfielders they deserve special mention:

One step to throw. There is no time to take several running steps before throwing back to the infield or to home plate, and in fact this often results in inaccurate throws. The outfielder should step out with his lead foot and fire the ball as well as he can with that motion. Quickness is essential.

Never hold the ball. No outfielder ever gained an advantage delaying his throw back to the infield. As noted above, before the ball is pitched he should have it in mind where he will go with the play if it is hit to him. He should be drilled into the habit of a quick throw back to the infield on every play.

One of the great infielders, and great ballplayers of all time, Jackie Robinson, was rarely called upon to play in the outfield, but he knew enough about it to comment about one fault that could lead to misplays. Robinson's advice to outfielders charging in on grounders was to run on the balls of the feet and not allow the heels to hit the ground. The heels hitting the ground will *jar the eyes* and make the ball appear to jump off line.

TRIM

" I'M NOT DELAYING THE GAME! THAT'S MY SLOW BALL."

For specially talented outfielders: There is a knack big leaguers have of taking fly balls when a runner is in position to advance after the catch, but it requires a level of confidence and ability that is rare in kids' play. The outfielder times his catch so that he is two steps behind the ball just before it comes down. He moves in, makes the catch and uses his momentum for the one step and throw. This adds tremendous velocity to the throw, compared to a standing start under the ball.

Catching the fly ball: The catch should be made at head height or slightly higher, using both hands, and *watching the ball into the glove.* The high-hand position gives the fielder a second chance at a bobbled ball before it hits the ground, and it is also a good preliminary position for starting a quick throw back to the infield.

Backing up the infield: Outfielders have to be alert at all times to back up infielders. On a slow roller or bunted ball leading to a play at first, the rightfielder should be moving into position behind the first baseman in case there is an overthrow. The centerfielder has the responsibility for cutting off a catcher's throw to second base that gets past the second baseman and shortstop. The leftfielder has a similar job behind the third baseman.

Practice daily: On days when there is no team practice or league game, an outfielder should get together with a teammate and practice catching fly balls and grounders, because the limited practice periods are not enough for a beginning player to achieve confidence at his job.

And confidence is the name of the game.

5. Coaching

Teaching Is Its Own Reward; Plans, Guidelines and Joy

The joy in coaching athletes, at any level, is the joy of seeing their improvement, season after season. It's only human that the coach believes *he* had a little something to do with that improvement.

For the coach of kid baseball this joy is compressed into a few happy weeks of summer. That youngster at second base—the one who had two left feet when summer began—now makes the backhand stab deep behind the base, comes up and plants his foot, makes the throw. In time! That's the kind of rewarding sight that makes life worth living, and makes grown men give up countless hours of their own, to transform children into baseball players.

Such transformations take place everywhere every season, to varying degrees, depending upon how much attention is paid to the job. It's sort of natural, like growing a garden. The coaching aids which follow are directly related to youngsters beginning baseball, not any other kind of baseball.

Few adults—and especially few adults who have already

volunteered to coach a team of youngsters—will confess to ignorance where the Grand Old Game is concerned. In a bygone generation this would be like doubting one's sanity. However, in the first place, few adults know as much baseball as they think they do, whether they ever played it or not. And a little knowledge is a dangerous thing. Ted Williams knew everything about hitting, but nothing at all about human nature, which is why he was a failure as a manager. Human nature may be what baseball is all about, and why those who love it love no other game as well. Ring Lardner got into this side of baseball with a great short story, "Harmony." There is the other side of the coin, too, that perhaps the average baseball fan has enough savvy to handle a major league team. Chicago White Sox owner Charley Comiskey proved this forever in 1915 when he whimsically offered a manager's job to his favorite tavern owner in Peoria, Ill. Clarence (Pants) Rowland proceeded in three years to manage the White Sox to a World Series victory over John McGraw's Giants.

All of this has nothing to do with the proposition at hand, coaching kid baseball. So many fine managerial moves—the sacrifice bunt, the hit-and-run, the intentional walk—are worthless strategy in the little game. The double play is a rarity. At every level of baseball, when there is one out and a runner on first, the cry goes up, "Get two, gang! Get two!" In kid baseball, the cry should be, "Get one—*then* two!"

But first, everything begins with the coach and commitment.

COACHING RESPONSIBILITY: Managing a kid baseball team is no casual, one-practice-a-week undertaking.

Game dates are appealing, where the maestro directs his players and a decision is on the line. It is too common a practice that a coach requires only one workout a week, sandwiched in between the league schedule. If a coach cannot devote the time to his team, he should decline the honor and let somebody else step forward to take the job. The worst that can happen is that the players will be dispersed around the league—to coaches who *do* have the time.

Two mandatory practices a week, other than game dates, is the ideal. In addition, there should be one, preferably two, voluntary days devoted entirely to batting practice. The word "voluntary" is of course a joke. These will be the best-attended practices. Who doesn't love to hit? The idea that youngsters can be worn out by too much of this kind of work is ludicrous. What can they have better to do with their spare moments than play baseball in the summertime?

Other than being there for enough practices every week to make a difference, the ideal coach would have two other physical attributes: He should be able to meet the ball with the bat; and he should be able to pitch batting practice.

There are two vital reasons for this double requirement. First, youngsters under thirteen understand the "show and tell" principle of teaching better than anybody. The demands on skill are elementary, but when a coach can demonstrate that a stop-action swing will send the ball singing, their eyes open wider. Second, throwing batting practice will place the coach in the best teaching position of all, the pitcher's mound. Furthermore, he is wonderfully neutral, erasing the competitiveness that will occur when one of the batter's peers is throwing the ball.

Finally, there is the all-important attitude, the approach to coaching these innocents. A fine balance must be drawn—no babying, treat them like adults, never forgetting they are children. In fact, more attention should be paid to the less-talented players on the team. The rewards for this in terms of play are surprising. The rewards for this, adult-to-youngster, are sure and enduring.

THE FIRST DAYS: In most cases, the best athlete will be the pitcher—a natural, with excellent coordination. If this Best One cannot pitch, perhaps due to lack of control, he will probably be best suited at shortstop. The next orders of priority are catcher, second base, first base, centerfield for speed, rightfield for fielding ability and arm. The best place to put an undeveloped player is leftfield, *because most young hitters hit late,* and most hitters are right-handed. This means the ball will go to the right of the diamond, and the second baseman and the rightfielder will be the most important defensive players.

Every kid will have a fixed idea where he wants to play, based on his heroes in the major leagues. Let him try out where he wants, then induce a change if necessary. A lefthander may have his heart set on playing shortstop. He can only play first base and outfield, and it is the coach's job to educate him.

After two days of practice, a coach should be able to spot the strong arms: the fellow he wants to try as a pitcher, the one he wants on third base, the good glove he wants on second, the speed he wants in centerfield, the take-charge and baseball-smart kid he wants behind the plate. Baseball is a stereotyped game in this regard and it is difficult to go wrong in typecasting. The trick is to sugarcoat the pill: "You have got such a great arm, I want you playing here, the team needs you here." If the kid who wants to be a second baseman has a great arm, he should be moved to third.

OPENING DRILLS: The beginning emphasis will be on fielding fundamentals because this is the phase of the kids' game that usually separates the winners from the losers. Assign each of your four infielders a partner who will stand on the baseline. The partners throwing to the first baseman and the second baseman will stand along the baseline between home plate and third base. The partners throwing to the third baseman and the shortstop will stand along the baseline between home plate and first. They will throw ground balls so the fielders will have to move laterally to reach them.

THE INFIELD: Infield fundamentals are few, but they must be drilled again and again:

Move to get the body in front of the ball. This does two things—it gets the fielder into position to use both his hands, and on a misplay the body will block the ball and keep it from getting through to the outfield for extra bases. Fear of getting hit by a baseball is natural, but it will finally be overcome after a kid gets hit a few times and discovers it doesn't hurt as much as he thought it would. Meanwhile, appeal to his pride: Baseball is a tough game, and it takes tough kids to play it. (The truth, of course, is that baseball is the least physical of all team sports.)

Field the ball with two hands. Aside from the obvious advantage of trapping a ball in the glove, this also brings the bare hand into position so the fielder can quickly set for his throw.

Get down to the ball. The fielder must flex his knees to bring his whole body near the level of the bouncing ball, not just his arms and hands. This position will also help on the most important fundamental of all:

Always watch the ball into the glove. A coach will have to repeat this homily until the kids are sick of hearing it. There are no easy chances in baseball, but there are easy chances made hard by taking the eyes off the ball.

Take one step in the direction of the throw. The greatest aid to throwing accuracy is proper foot movement. It brings the body in balance. Coaches are forever amazed at the tendency of youngsters to take a side step with the leading foot as they throw. Thus are scatter-arms born. One step in the direction of the throw also helps the next fundamental:

Never hurry a throw. After a fielder comes up with the ball, he must plant his back foot to anchor his body in perfect balance. *Then* he makes the throw, taking one step in the direction of the target, keeping his eye on the target, and following through with his body.

THE OUTFIELD: While the infield drill is going on, outfielders should be paired off with one group along the leftfield line and the others in center and rightcenter field—throwing fly balls and ground balls to each other. The emphasis here is on lateral movement, getting the body in front of the ball, watching the ball into the glove, making the catch at all times with two hands. On fly balls, the catch should be made at head level, with glove fingers up and palm outward. The other fundamentals:

Play deep and come up to the ball. The hardest play for an outfielder to make, even in the major leagues, is on a ball hit over his head. A talented player can be taught to judge a fly ball and catch it moving forward so that his momentum will help the power of his throw. This trick is usually beyond the ability of a youngster.

Touch right knee to ground when fielding all ground balls. (Lefthanders should touch left knee to ground.) Even with runners on base, the most important job for the outfielder is making sure the ball doesn't get past him. In kid baseball a ball that bounds past an outfielder usually results in the batter circling the bases. The kids even call this a home run. As will be noted below in a section on strategy, most losses are the results of big innings aided by errors and bases on balls.

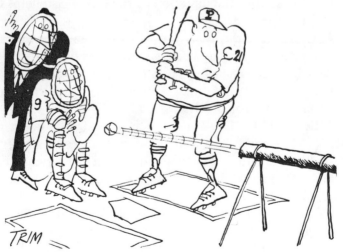

"WOW! RIGHT DOWN THE PIPE...STRIIIKE ONE!"

Take one step and throw. Quickness in getting the ball back to the infield is as important as the strength of an outfielder's throwing arm. An outfielder should never hold the ball for any reason, or "bluff" a throw, or run in with it toward the infield. The one-step throw, getting rid of the ball as fast as he can get the body in balanced control, is essential. Most youngsters will develop on their own the "back foot hop" that precedes the step and adds momentum to the throw.

Move with every pitch. An outfielder should "stay in the game" by moving lightly onto the balls of his feet with each pitch. He should learn to lean and move to his left slightly when the pitch is on the outside of the plate, to his right when the pitch is inside. He should get a relay signal from the shortstop or second baseman when the pitcher is going to throw an off-speed pitch. He should be aware that a righthand batter will hit an inside pitch or an off-speed pitch to the third base side of the diamond. This leaning movement helps outfielders "get a jump on the ball," that is, begin moving in the direction the ball is likely to be hit even before it is hit.

Keep all throws low. This is especially important on throws to home plate, which should come in on one bounce. High-arched throws tend to be erratic and often miss connections with both the infielder and his backup man.

PITCHING: Usually, the team's best athlete will be its ace pitcher. It's a matter of sorting out the most well-coordinated youngsters and giving them a trial on the mound. At this age *size* is an important factor. The larger a boy is the harder he can be taught to throw, *safely*. Youngsters of slight build, especially the ones with plenty of competitiveness, are in danger of hurting their arms permanently from trying to pitch harder than their young bodies will allow.

But the overriding primary quality in a young pitcher is *control*. Give preference to the kid who can throw strikes, over a teammate who can throw harder. The Dodgers kept Sandy Koufax on their team for six seasons before he became a winning pitcher—but a youngster's summer is short and time is fleeting. It is possible, however, that a young fireballer can be taught enough control to be an effective pitcher before the schedule is over.

The emphasis on control is classic, dating from the deathbed statement of Manager George Stallings, whose 1914 "Miracle Braves" came from last place on July 4 to win the pennant for Boston and then win the World Series. When Stallings died years later, he spoke for all managers everywhere when his last words were: "Bases on balls killed me." And bases on balls will surely hurt a kid team. A coach wants to make the opposition swing at strikes, betting that the other team hasn't had as much batting practice as his club has had.

The following fundamentals include ways to increase a pitcher's firepower and his control:

No wind-up. Youngsters will want to emulate the high kick of Juan Marichal, or the windmill and extreme body turn of some other major league hero. They should be reminded that Don Larsen of the New York Yankees pitched the only perfect game in World Series history without a windup. Seasoned pitchers have worked out their own individual styles through years of trial and error. So will the average youngster. But, first, he has to start with the basic idea—get the ball over the plate. A righthanded pitcher should face the plate squarely, with his right foot on the rubber and his left foot slightly behind, both hands at his belly button, eyes forever on the catcher's mitt. From that stance he goes into his normal throwing motion, determined to throw a strike.

Push off strong. This is how a youngster with little power and good control can boost his power-rating. A kid who already throws hard will soon be throwing "smoke" when he learns the knack of using the pitcher's slab. That's why it is there, to give a pitcher the solid platform he needs to propel his body, arm and the ball toward the plate. Use it. For a righthander the strength in his right leg, pushing off against the slab, will have as much to do with his fast ball as his right arm will. This importance of leg strength is the reason major league pitchers run in the outfield on their off days, along with the necessity to build stamina.

Step in direct line to the catcher's mitt. No pitcher can throw strikes with power if his leading foot is off line. It may be necessary to have the pitcher watch his foot as it comes down when he throws to the plate.

Follow through. The body should come around with the arm motion. This seems elemental, but too many youngsters try to pitch with "all arm," neglecting to bring the shoulder and hip and upper torso around behind the pitch. They can even be effective for a while, but the neglect is dangerous for their arms and robs them of the best fast balls.

Never throw a curve. There is absolutely no reason a subteen ballplayer should ever attempt to throw a curve ball. There is a wealth of medical evidence that this is harmful to the tender and growing elbow joint. There is an easy substitute pitch for the curve, serving the same purpose, without any risk:

The beginner's change-up. Even young batters when fed a steady diet of fast balls will soon begin teeing off on the pitch. The answer is the off-speed delivery. It should only be used against the opposition's best hitters—a below-average hitter will be delighted to see a pitch coming in at a speed he can handle. In the major leagues a change-up is thrown with the ball shoved into the back of the hand, which is why it is often called "the palm ball." The baseball used in kid leagues, slightly smaller than regulation, is still too large for the normal youngster's hand. The same effect can result from gripping the ball with the first three fingers, as far back in the hand as possible, going through the same arm motion as if delivering a fast ball—then letting up, either at the moment of release, or earlier. Each youngster will work out the style that best suits him. The point is to take about 15-20 percent off the speed of the pitch. Not 50 percent. A too slow change-up allows the batter to reset his timing.

Daily practice. Pitchers should have a half-hour session with a catcher, whether it's at team practice or in their backyard with father, brother or neighborhood pal, every day. There is one simple rule that will get across the main emphasis of the workout: the pitcher has to throw two strikes before he can try any other kind of pitch or fanciful delivery. Maybe he'll want to experiment with a sidearm "crossfire," even a submarine pitch or his version of the knuckleball. Fine. But first he has to throw two strikes.

CATCHING: The model kid catcher has an outgoing, talkative personality, a quick mind and self-confidence. It would also be great if he had a powerful arm, but quickness and accuracy can make up for that shortcoming, and those assets can be taught.

"WHAT'S THE RULE IF IT DOESN'T COME DOWN?"

The catcher must perform as the team's defensive quarterback, stepping in front of the plate to remind teammates that there are two outs, or to remind them where the batter hit the ball his last time up. On throws home from the outfield, he must make the call to the cut-off man whether to intercept the ball and try for the batter advancing to second or let it go through for an attempted putout at the plate. In short, the catcher has to be a live wire.

The fundamentals of catching are few but absolute:

Positioning. To most youngsters the "scariest" part of the catcher's job is that he must work so close to a swinging bat. But he must position himself as close as possible to the batter, for two reasons: (1) Safety. The further away from the bat he is, the more likely he is to get hit by a foul tip. A catcher who backs off to a "safe" distance will find himself reaching with his bare hand, fingers extended, in an automatic reflex action. Close in, there's no time for the reflex. (2) The close position assures the pitcher that his strikes will be called where they are pitched, rather than where they are caught. Umpires, even the ones in the major leagues, are influenced by the position of the mitt when the ball reaches it.

The crouch. When there are no men on base, the catcher can be permitted to use the stance that is most comfortable for him—the full squat, one knee on the ground, or anyway at all.

With men on base, he should be in a low crouch with his left foot half a stride in front of his right, offering his mitt as a target right over the center of the plate just below the batter's waistline.

Avoiding broken fingers. Until the ball reaches the mitt, the catcher's right hand must be closed in a "loose fist" with the thumb pressing against the first joint of the forefinger. Extended fingers draw foul tips like magnets, and then it's off to splintsville.

The quick throw. The test of a catcher's arm is his ability to get the ball to second base, but the most powerful arm will have no chance at beating the runner if the two basics of quickness are not learned: (1) The throw should begin from just behind the right ear. It's a snap throw, not a full arm extension. There is no time to bring the ball back of the body to throw normally. (2) Take one step, directly toward second base, and throw. The back foot should remain planted from the time the ball is caught. These two basics will rob the catcher of his normal throwing power, until repetition gradually brings improvement. But they reinforce the main goal, accuracy.

It doesn't matter if the throw bounces on its way to second base, as long as it is on line. A throw that sails over the heads of the shortstop and second baseman too often results in the runner coming all the way home. And in no time at all—using the one step and the snap throw from behind the ear—a young catcher will be firing nothing but bullseyes.

"Blocking" the plate. On a close play at home, the catcher should place his left foot exactly on the baseline and be squared away to receive the throw in a balanced position. Placing the left foot on the baseline, rather than straddling the baseline with the body, will invite the runner to slide, because he can see the back half of home plate. But it also means he has to slide *around* the catcher to reach it. Once the catcher has the ball in his mitt he is in good position to shift his body into the runner.

HITTING: Baseball scouts want to know mainly two things about a prospect before offering him a contract: Can he run, can he throw? They regard speed afoot and a powerful arm as God-given, and no amount of coaching will improve either. It is not until these two requirements are met that they turn to a third: Can he hit with power? A youngster who has attained his full growth, or close to it, and still hits singles will forever hit singles.

But it's notable that nobody worries about whether a prospect is a hitter. That's because *hitting can be taught.* More to the point here, *hitting can be learned.* Where kid players are concerned, once they have been told the basic principles of hands and stance and stride, it is learned through repetition. That means batting practice, and lots of it.

Quite a few major league players and managers have taken critical stands against the kids' version of the game, and they all lead off their arguments with the same complaint: The kids don't get enough chances to hit. Harry (The Hat) Walker, onetime National League batting champion and currently hitting coach for the St. Louis Cardinals, says, "There's only one way for a kid to learn how to hit—by swinging a bat. That's where little leagues fail. A kid goes to bat once or twice a game, then he is taken out and another kid gets a chance to play."

Yogi Berra, manager of the New York Mets, agrees with Walker. "That's what's happening to baseball," he says. "There are no hitters being developed, because the kids don't hit enough."

Therefore, the first rule in teaching hitting is:

Batting practice. The coach should do the pitching, with two helpers, one to catch balls thrown back by the fielders and the other to hand balls to the coach. The helpers should be stationed right behind the pitcher's mound so the coach can knock down any balls hit back through the middle.

From the first day of practice there may be several boys who seem to be doing everything wrong and still manage to sock the ball all over the place. They should be left alone. Refinements can be added later to increase their power or consistency.

Extended batting practice—three or four times a week and thirty to forty chances at each practice—is a guaranteed way to overcome the top handicap for most beginning hitters, fear of the baseball. Hitting practice pitches increases confidence and the joy in hitting that enable a youngster to "hang in there" in real competition. Also, he may get hit a few times and discover the world didn't come to an end.

Switch hitting. A coach has a wonderful opportunity, particularly with fledgling batters who have rarely held a bat in their hands before, to convert youngsters into lefthanded batters and switch hitters. Every one of the more talented hitters, and a few of the least talented, should be made to try a few swings from the opposite side of the plate. This will be a tremendous bonus for them the rest of their baseball careers. When they begin to see curve balls, the ball will always be breaking into them and easier to hit. A lefthanded batter has the additional advantage of being a step-and-a-half closer to first base when he hits the ball.

Watch the ball hit the bat. It should be drilled into the kid ballplayer again and again that he must concentrate on the ball from the first moment he can see it, just before the pitcher's release, and watch it all the way until it meets his bat. If he's not swinging, he should watch it into the catcher's mitt. This rule will cure a number of beginners' flaws—such as closing the eyes when swinging, or flinching the head away from the plate. "You can't hit what you can't see," the kids should be told. And, "If you take your eyes off the ball, you're swinging at air. Nobody ever got any basehits hitting air."

Stroke the ball. This phrase best describes the goal of a smooth, level swing designed to deliver line drives. It should be repeated as much as possible that line drives often become home runs in kid baseball when they land between the outfielders. Even in the major leagues, players forget this principle from time to time. Says Home Run King Henry Aaron, "I never swing any different for a basehit than for a home run. The home runs just happen when you're swinging good."

The coach should demonstrate with a "stop-action" swing how much will happen if the batter simply meets the ball with the bat. The swing should be stopped at the point of contact, just in front of the plate, while the student stands opposite, just across the batter's box. His eyes will grow big and round when he sees how the ball jumps off the bat when met squarely.

The Johnny Bench stance. As noted above, if the kid is hitting the baseball, the coach should be very hesitant about changing his stance or his style. But for kids who have no idea about what they are doing, the best model is the orthodox example of the great Cincinnati catcher. Bench stands with his feet spread just beyond shoulder width, lined up parallel to the flight of the ball. His upper body is tilted only slightly forward, because that's where he wants his weight to be—forward—when he makes contact with the ball. His hands are together, gripping the bat *tightly*, and the key to his hand position is that his upper right arm is straight out in a line from his shoulder and *parallel to the ground*. The hands are comfortably away from the body, and the bat is pointing *straight up at the sky*.

From this position several good things begin to happen when Bench starts his swing. His front foot is ready to "step into" the ball. The high position of his right elbow ensures he won't be cutting *up* at the ball and he has less tendency to miss the ball altogether by swinging *below* the flight. All batters, and kid players especially, swing below the ball 90 percent of the time.

(One year at spring training the Cincinnati Reds had their players fire BB guns at the top half of cardboard disks. This emphasized a popular hitting principle, aim for the top half of the ball, but this is too fine a point for twelve-year-olds and younger.)

Position in the batter's box. The speed of the opposing pitcher is normally the critical factor to the young hitter. So he should stand as deep in the batter's box as the lines allow. He should also stand as close to the plate as the lines allow. Beginning hitters won't like this advice, but there is a very good reason for it. Home plate is the only dimension in a Little League park that is the same as in a major league park—17 inches. The batter's box is 2 inches closer (4 inches vs. 6 inches), but this still doesn't make up for shorter Little League bats and Little League physiques. An average-size youngster will have a difficult time reaching an outside pitch unless he is "crowding the plate."

Foot action, and "stepping in the bucket." When a player is told to "step into" the pitch, it means simply this: On an outside pitch he should step with his front foot in the direction of first base. On a pitch over the center of the plate he should step straight ahead toward second base. On an inside pitch he does the same, or at most in the direction of the shortstop.

Many a youngster will want to move his front foot completely away from the plate to keep his body from getting hit by a baseball. This is known as "bailing out" or trying to put a foot in the water bucket, which is in the dugout. The easiest way to cure this is to place a bat on the ground, pointing toward the pitcher's mound and about 12 inches from his front foot. It should be toward the front of the batter's box where he can see it in the corner of his vision as he looks at the pitcher's mound.

The back foot should *stay home* at all times during the swing. A fiddle-footed hitter will never make contact with the baseball. As he swings the bat, his weight will normally shift from his back foot to his front foot. This isn't something he should be told about unless the coach sees that it's a specific problem.

Curing a hitch. A "hitch" in the swing is simply the player dropping his hands low and bringing them up again to begin his stroke. It results, at best, in uppercutting the baseball. A persistent hitch can be partially corrected by widening the player's stance; the lowering of the hands is always in time with the stride of the front foot.

BUNTING: This is a department unto itself, because it is the easiest way to "get the ball in play," especially when the least-talented hitters are at the plate.

A bunted ball, more often than not, creates havoc in the infield.That is its purpose, to make something happen.

The sacrifice bunt (a beloved part of "percentage

baseball") is of no value at the kid baseball level. Outs are too precious there.

The telegraphed bunt. Not one major leaguer in twenty can properly execute the drag bunt or the delayed bunt, so it is folly to teach kids anything but the easiest way to get the bat on the ball. The first move is a step to the left with the front foot, bringing the right foot forward and the body in a squared-away position facing the pitcher. This double move is made the minute the pitcher begins his motion. The left hand grips the bat at the knob end, the right hand grips the back half of the bat, even with the trademark, with the thumb on top and the fingertips underneath. The knees should be flexed as the bunter awaits the pitch. The bat remains horizontal at all times, as the hitter will crouch low to reach a low pitch or raise up to meet a high pitch. The bat is placed on the ball with a slight nudge.

" SETTLE DOWN ... YOU'RE GETTING WILD."

A bunting drill should be the extended part of every batting practice. Soon even the most ineffective hitters will be able to bunt with precision.

Do *not* allow youngsters to lean over the bat as it makes contact with the ball. This leads to dental bills. In fact, one of the advantages of the always-horizontal bat position is that the kids don't tip fouls into their bodies, as they might do with the bat in a slanted position.

The two-strike rule. It should be automatic, no matter how talented the hitter, that every batter should choke up on the bat when the count reaches two strikes against him. The motto is: "Choke up on the bat and meet the ball!"

ADVANCED INFIELD PRACTICE: After the beginning days, when infielders were thrown ground balls by their partners, the coach will conduct the standard infield practice, hitting grounders and calling out, "Get one!" (a throw to first) or "Get two!" (a throw to second and relay to first). In either case the first baseman then throws the ball to the catcher, the catcher throws to the boy or girl who fielded the ball, and then the throw comes back home.

Later on in the season, as the infield becomes more adept, there is an "advanced infield drill" that will make the kids feel like pros. (Kid baseball is supposed to be fun. Remember?) It requires two first basemen and two catchers. Say it begins with a grounder to third. As soon as the third baseman comes up with the ball and starts his throw to first, the coach hits the next ground ball to the shortstop. The first first baseman is making a throw to the catcher as the second first baseman takes the shortstop's throw. The catcher throws to the third baseman and gets it back again. The second catcher is taking the second first baseman's throw and firing down to the shortstop at second base and he fires it back home again. Meanwhile, when the shortstop had begun his throw to first, the coach had hit a ground ball to the second baseman. And around it goes.

DEFENSIVE STRATEGY: The basic defensive idea in kid baseball can be stated in one sentence: *Get the one sure out.* Even if it means giving up a run, or allowing another runner to advance into scoring position. The big inning is what wins games, and getting the one sure out avoids letting the other side have a big inning.

The backup. There is an almost endless series of backup combinations which must be drilled so the team can avoid another prime cause of a big inning; the shortstop and the second baseman back each other up on all throws into the second base area. On a ground ball when there are no men on base, the catcher runs down the line to back up the first baseman. On a base hit to the outfield with a man on first, the pitcher backs up the third baseman. On a bunted ball down the third base side, the right fielder should be moving up in case the third baseman overthrows first. On an attempted steal of second, the centerfielder should also be moving in fast in case the catcher's throw gets through to the outfield. On a basehit to the outfield with a man on second, the pitcher should back up the catcher.

This backup protection is vital. It should definitely be included in "Game Awards" (see below).

The cutoff play. This is one of the surest ways to stifle a big inning by the opposition. It occurs when a baserunner is heading for home, the throw is coming in from the outfield, and the hitter is rounding first, expecting to take an easy second base while the catcher attempts a putout at the plate. But the cutoff man (normally the first baseman) is lined up with the throw, halfway into the infield. The catcher has the whole play in front of him so he makes the call: "Let it go! Let it go!" or "Cut it off! Cut if off!" Whereupon the cutoff man intercepts the throw and fires to second for a sure putout.

" JUST HOW LONG HAVE YOU BEEN STRANDED HERE ON SECOND BASE? "

In ballparks where the seating sections are built close to the foul lines, and there's no real room for a backup man behind either first base or home plate, the pitcher can be used as the cutoff man.

The run-down. When a runner is caught between bases—and this frequently happens in kid baseball—the defensive team should follow one basic rule: The ball must never be thrown more than twice. The fielder with the ball must run down the baseline at the runner, until the runner makes a decision what he's going to do. Once the runner commits himself, the first throw is made. Never more than two.

OFFENSIVE STRATEGY: Only on rare occasions should there be an order to "take" a pitch. One such would be a close game with men on base, a below-average hitter at the plate, and the count 3-0. But if the team's top hitter is at the plate in the same situation, he should rip away.

There is no glory in a base on balls, and hitting is the joy of the game. So the batter should go up to the plate determined to "be a hitter." He should be poised to go for the first pitch if it's in his strike zone.

Running the bases. The subtleties of this subject have been erased in the Little League organization by a rule that prohibits a baserunner from leaving his base until the ball has crossed the plate, but there is still plenty of room for hustle.

The batter who drives the ball into the outfield should start out thinking about getting to second base. When he gets within 15 feet of first base he will veer to the right about 3 or 4 feet, hit the bag with his left foot and head for second—until the first base coach yells, "Hold it!" The first base coach (the coaches will be the team's baseball-smart-twelve-year-olds) is in a cooler position to decide whether the runner should go for two. Similarly, it will be the third base coach's decision on sending a runner home from second on a base hit. This leaves the runner with only one thing on his mind—running!

The psychology of play opens up two opportunities that

might never be considered at other levels of the game: (1) Going from first to third on a ground ball hit to the third baseman. This fellow will normally be so elated at making his throw to first for a putout on the hitter that he'll neglect to cover third base. Even if he does, the play requires he make a good recovery getting back to the bag and it requires the first baseman to make a heads-up and perfect throw to third. (2) If the runner on second has good speed, he can come all the way home on a bunted ball which is fielded and thrown to first base. This is taking advantage of innocence, but they are all in the game together.

" ADMIT IT, FARLEY, ...THAT WAS A GRAND SLAM TO END ALL GRAND SLAMS."

THE TEAM IDEA: Here is an idea where a coach can put his personal stamp on a team, instill pride, and drive home the truism that "team play" can produce victories over other teams who may have greater individual talents.

Following are some precepts, tips and disciplines that have worked down through the years:

It ought to be a team rule that no player comes to practice alone. He should arrange to bring a teammate with him, or catch a ride himself with one or more teammates.

Never a discouraging word. No coach can tolerate criticism within the team ("You shoulda had that, Ricky!")

Keep the bench happy. The more practices a coach schedules, including practice games, the less complaints he'll have about playing the best nine kids until a game is no longer in doubt. The kids themselves will know who should be playing. Bench riders should be told they have a responsibility to keep a good attitude, or their grumbling will erode a team. Communication helps. A coach should work the hardest with his least-talented players. He should look for spots to use his fastest sub as a pinch-runner, for instance.

Keep the bench disciplined. The players should have designated spots on the bench when the team is at bat, outfielders with outfielders, infielders with infielders. *And baseball talk only.* When the opposing team is taking pregame batting practice, the players should be on the bench paying attention to the weaknesses and strengths of the opponents.

Team outings. Early in the season the team ought to be gathered together for an exercise in togetherness—a trip to see a professional game, or an American Legion game, or even another kid baseball game. If there is a nearby batting cage (pitching machine), the team can go in a group and hit for a Coke. (Pitching machines are fine for helping a batter whose timing is off, but of little value as a regular substitute for live batting practice.) The purpose of these outings is to impress the idea they are a team, all friends together.

Never substitute for a player in the middle of an inning. There has never been a World Series worth this kind of humiliation to a twelve-year-old.

Make "Game Awards." Have a statistician keep a scorer's sheet on the game, including backups on overthrows and top defensive plays. Give an award to the top hitter or hitters, to the best fielding gem, and to the fellow who made the most backup stops. It doesn't matter what these awards are in value. In many parts of the country it's a tradition that parents rotate bringing the postgame soft drinks. Many coaches give the top hitter a "First Coke" award, which means while the coach is still going over the game with the rest of the team, this worthy strolls up to the soft drink bucket and quenches his thirst in honored grandeur. If a pitcher throws a shutout, award him the "Game Ball" complete with signatures by his teammates.

Encouraging chatter. The players in the field should be in constant communication with one another—calling around the number of outs, where the next play is going, what the hitter is likely to do. And they should be encouraging the pitcher all the way. But the players in the field shouldn't distract themselves with jockeying opponents—yelling "Swing!" at the batter, for instance. The subs on the bench can handle this department. That's why they call them bench jockeys.

There is only one final rule for a coach: Pray, for patience.

PART II

PART II

6. Thank Heaven for Little Girls

How to Make Up for a Late Start

There was a time, not too long ago, when the paths marked out for girls and boys were separate and distinct. Boys played at being cowboys, doctors, detectives—even baseball players—and girls played at being housewives, nurses, teachers—but not ball players. Life was simpler then. Perhaps not better, just simpler.

So when the women's movement for equality took on organized kid baseball, it was natural that there would be a mighty fuss. Those who ran the game were raised with a traditional understanding of separate roles, and games, for boys and girls. One could go along with equal pay—but a girl stealing second base?

The "men only" rules of McSorley's Wonderful Saloon could be voided, the tables down at Maury's could be invaded. But not baseball, the last bastion this side of the Men's Room. The lines of defense were erected—and knocked down one by one:

Do you want your girl to grow up and chew tobacco? This one didn't work when somebody reported that, aside from a declining number of managers and coaches, few major leaguers chew anything stronger than bubblegum.

Cancerous lesions may form due to physical impact on the breast tissue. This argument was thrown out at first when no medical authority could produce figures to substantiate the notion.

Well, then, how about cosmetic damage? A bad hop could render a future beauty queen snaggle-toothed forever. A separatist put the question to Mrs. Betty Hoadley of New Jersey, whose daughter Kristen, eleven, wanted to be a pitcher for a kid baseball team. "Who would you rather lose some teeth that way, your daughter or your son?" And Mrs. Hoadley replied, "Either one. They are equal human beings." What are you going to do with a woman like that?

What you are going to do, it turns out, is let her daughter play—if she can get the high, hard one over the plate as well as the next player.

The national headquarters of Little League had fended off all arguments in the controversy, merely pointing out that it was the only sports group in the country established by Federal charter, a vote of the Congress, and that charter specified "boys only," the same as the Boy Scouts of America.

But baseball, like other institutions, found itself confronted with changing attitudes. Mothers and fathers everywhere were saying, "You can't ban my little girl," and taking the case to the courts. The number of cases initiated, as well as the number of rulings favorable to the girls' position—the Supreme Court sided with a girl from New Jersey—seemed to mark an end to official opposition. Whether Little League officials cooperate fully or not, girls are in baseball to stay. Like boys, they will be judged for their ability to play kid baseball, and not on an irrelevant notion of some coach.

by Jeff Millar & Bill Hinds

What had been lost sight of through all of this wild talk and recrimination was brought back into perspective by a former major league pitcher, Dallas Green, who just happened to have a daughter named Kimberly who wanted in the game. "For kids under twelve," Green said, "baseball should be fun for everybody, so it shouldn't matter if girls play."

"Fun," of course, is the ideal, with the added proviso that the more skill you have the more fun baseball is. And if anyone thought the advent of girls would erode competitiveness from the small-fry's game, he was soon put straight by a couple of nationally publicized incidents. When shortstop Cathy Arnold was sidelined by Little League officials in Arkansas, she watched from the bench as her replacement booted two grounders and went 0-for-3 at bat. Said Cathy: "He can't catch the ball like I can, and he can't hit like I can. I think he ought to go sit down."

No bench-rider in the major leagues could have put the issue any straighter than that.

An eleven-year-old pitcher from West Virginia made a comment which best sums what kid baseball is about. Bunny Parker threw a no-hit game past an all-boy team. "They yelled at me and called me a monkey, and things like that," Bunny said, "but I didn't care. The boys on my team are proud of me."

Okay, now that the issue has been shredded, what about the nitty-gritty of the subject:

Can girls play kid baseball on the same level as the boys? The answer is, from the standpoint of muscle and bone and maturity, girls are better equipped to play baseball through ages up to twelve years. School systems in

California, Illinois and New Jersey (among others) have kept track of student development through the preteen and next few years. Up to age twelve, girls are slightly *ahead* of boys in physical capacity. At age thirteen the boys catch up and quickly begin to increase their bodily superiority in terms of strength and stamina and speed. So, the average ten-to twelve-year–old girl when matched against the *average* boy of that age definitely won't be conceding anything and, in fact, will enjoy a slight edge.

What makes some girls look awkward when they try to throw or run or hit? They have never had a chance to learn, and certainly have never been shown, how to do these things right. Most little girls simply have never played "catch" in the backyard as their brothers have done since age four or five. This is their only handicap, and the idea that pelvic structure limits their physical talents is nothing but an old wives' tale. Simply by repetition, girls can learn how to run-throw-hit-catch the same way boys do, in stepladder fashion:

Start with a softball and a softball glove. This is the way 90 percent of the young boys begin the game. The beginning principles are the same, and early success leads to enthusiasm. Choke up on the bat. Try to watch the ball hit the bat. Discover that getting hit by a ball doesn't hurt that much. After a summer or two of softball, kids will find out a few things on their own—that a baseball is easier to throw than a softball, because they can get a better grip on it; and with a good glove it is also easier to catch. Hitting is another matter, but that can be an acquired talent, too.

A key to throwing. Since Old England invented the

game of "rounders," little girls have been hooted off of playing fields because their throwing efforts brought laughter. The little girls didn't mind. They consoled themselves: "I'm not *supposed* to know how to throw a ball." This is all ridiculous, of course. Girls throw "funny" for a very simple reason: *They don't move their feet.* Boys have the same trouble when they begin to throw, but they do so much throwing at an early age that they become adept through repetition. But it is an easy matter to teach any youngster to throw, at first by rote. A righthander should take one step with the left foot as the ball is brought to throwing position (comfortable, at an arm angle halfway between straight overhead and straight sidearm, called "the three-quarter motion"). Then, as the throwing motion is made, the right foot must be brought forward until it ends up forward of the left foot after the ball is released. This movement of the feet gets the whole right side of the body, plus the turn of the hips, into the

throw. Repetition will bring a smooth, fluid motion and great accuracy. The right foot should always be placed in the direction of the target.

Why girls can't run. Again, there is no inherent reason why girls can't run with the same efficient ground-eating grace that boys do. The trouble is, *they don't move their arms.* Some girls have a tendency to hold their arms straight down at their sides, or otherwise motionless, when running. Once they are taught to bend the arms at the elbows, so that the forearms are parallel to the ground at the beginning of a stride, then they will settle into the natural rhythm of forward and backward thrust. They don't have to be told that the right arm goes forward with the left foot and vice versa. The correct motion will evolve.

Hitting the ball. The basic instructions for hitting will be found in that chapter in this book, and also in the coaching chapter. In fact, all the instructions apply to both boys and girls. There is one hitting aid that should be used

by Jeff Millar & Bill Hinds

for girls who are just being introduced to a ball and a bat. That is the batting tee, available at any sporting goods store. The tee sits on home plate or any other level surface, positioning the ball at waist height, and this helps in teaching the one vital rule in hitting, *Watch the ball meet the bat.*

Special fielding drills for base-running and throwing. A batting tee can be useful in starting a drill that brings all the infield into play, and sometimes the outfield, too. With fielders in position, the batter hits the ball off the batting tee and begins running the bases. The fielders must throw the ball to first, then second, then third and then home before the batter makes it around all the bases. With beginning players, this often results in a dead heat, and the whole thing is fun, as well as good practice.

Special throwing drill for beginners. To learn the basic fundamentals of throwing, including use of the fully extended arm and the wrist movement at point of release, beginners should be throwing a ball against a wall. First a tennis ball could be used, then a softball and finally a baseball. They should throw at a waist-high target from distances up to 60 feet, the distance between the bases in kid baseball. The advantage of throwing against a wall is that the wall never misses, and it returns all throws, bad or not. This kind of practice allows the thrower to concentrate on fundamental movements.

With practice, and an environment at school and home that encourages girls' participation in sports, girls will be able to compete equally with boys in kid baseball. Once it's realized that the barriers are social, not physical, then the girls who wish to play will be able to play.

PART III

7. The Early Achievers

Joey Jay and Boog Powell

It may not have been quite as elevating as, say, being the first Mickey Mouse Club graduates to make it on Broadway, but it was close. The names are Joey Jay and Boog Powell, and they occupy a special place in the pantheon of kid baseball heroes.

Joseph Richard Jay, tall, darkly handsome, twice a twenty-game winner with the Cincinnati Reds, was the first Little League alumnus to reach the majors. He got there in 1953, with the Milwaukee Braves, a *wunderkind* of seventeen, only five years removed from his starring role for King's Gas Station.

John Wesley Powell, blond, beefy, looking like the anchor man in a circus trapeze act, was the first to bring off the World Series double—to start in a championship series at both levels. As the strongman of a Baltimore team that became a perennial contender beginning in the mid-sixties, Boog was the model first baseman. He had the build and the power and a neck the size of an average man's thigh.

And therein lies a small irony. Boog Powell, who was

designed to play first base, began his kid baseball career as a pitcher. And, yes, you guessed it, Joey Jay, whose arm kept him in the big leagues for thirteen years, started life as a first baseman. As they say, only in America.

For reasons clearly beyond his, and their, control, Joey Jay has become Little League's most historic figure. It isn't only that he was the first to come to national attention. It is, partly, that Joey Jay was so right for the assignment. More than a quarter century later, we still can't imagine any other name doing what he did. Joey Jay *sounds* like the first Little Leaguer to make it to the big leagues.

The kids' program had leaped beyond the boundaries of Pennsylvania in 1948, and spread into New England. In Middletown, Conn., twelve-year old Joey Jay tried out for the team sponsored by King's Gas Station, and managed by Mr. King, himself. "I can remember how excited we were," Joey says, rolling back the years. "It was all we could talk about. We used to play all the time on the back lots, but there was no discipline and you were lucky if you had five guys. It was an exciting thing to try out, to be a part of it, to play in an organized league with real bats and gloves and an honest to goodness ball.

"I played first base that year. At the time they had a rule that twelve-year olds couldn't pitch. We played a twelve-game season and, I'm probably exaggerating, but it seems to me I hit somewhere close to .400 and I had two home runs. I remember the home runs because one of them won the all-star game. And after the game they took us to the local drug store, where the druggist gave a free milk shake to anyone hitting a home run. So I went by and collected mine.

"We played on the same baseball diamond that the town team played on. They just shortened the bases when we played. I can recall during the middle of the season, we went out knocking on doors, trying to raise money for uniforms. The sponsor provided the equipment, balls and bats, and we brought our own gloves. It was the first year, and we were just getting off the ground."

You can picture Joey Jay at twelve, the all-star first baseman, polite, intent, mature for his age, a glimpse of the man he would soon become. It was the beginning of a productive career in baseball, influenced in a subtle way, which is the best way, by his father.

"My dad had quite a long pro career," he says. "He was with the old Boston Braves for a cup of coffee and he kicked around the minor leagues for a number of years. After that he went into industrial baseball, and one of his teammates one year was Jimmy Piersall. Jimmy was still in high school in Waterbury (Conn.), and he played the outfield. Those were fast, semipro leagues and every roster had its share of ex-pros.

"Jimmy was quite a character even then. He was only sixteen or seventeen, and big crowds came out just to see him. I was about ten then, but I can remember when the Philadelphia A's came to town for an exhibition game, and a reporter asked Connie Mack what he thought of Jimmy, because he was so popular in our area. It was pretty apparent, we thought, that he would become a big star. In a nice way Mr. Mack indicated that he wasn't very impressed. But not long after that, Jimmy made it to the big leagues.

"I was determined to make it in pro ball because of my

dad. But I gave him credit for one thing. He didn't interfere with my progress or try to force me at all. I felt no pressure in that respect, and I believe his attitude helped me. Of course, he was available whenever I went to him, but he was smart enough not to push me."

Jay came along at a time when the traditional, prewar patterns of baseball were changing. New bonus rules were turning the sport upside down, and the emergence of kid leagues had the scouts keeping a dizzy pace. They were practically raiding Maypole parties, looking for talent. No longer were the players starting at salaries that went up in pennies, spending long years of apprenticeship in the minors, waiting for someone on the big club to retire, or break a leg, then arriving as a nearly polished performer.

By the time he was fifteen, Joey Jay was pitching for money in the summer vacation leagues that sprang up in the resorts around Vermont and New Hampshire. The morning after his high school graduation, at seventeen, he flew to Milwaukee for a tryout with the Braves, recently transplanted from Boston. "I stayed there a week," he recalls, "and played in about three games with other kids they were working out. I was primarily an outfielder, but I can remember pitching batting practice under the eye of Bucky Walters, the pitching coach, who had started his career as a third baseman and then moved to the mound. At that time the Braves were as impressed with my hitting as the fact that I could throw hard. But it wasn't long before they decided my future was as a pitcher."

His career began with the Braves. He appeared in three games and won his only start in the summer of '53, not yet eighteen. And it ended with the Braves, by then in Atlanta, the arm gone, 0 and 4 the final weeks of the 1966 season. In between were the glory years with the Redlegs, seventy-five victories in less than six seasons, and their only victory (over Ralph Terry) in a losing World Series to the Yankees in 1961.

Jay was an impressive specimen at 6-4 and 228, a smooth righthander with a snapping fast ball. On occasion, a columnist or magazine writer would rediscover his status as Little League's pathfinder, and his teammates would give him the needle. "They used to refer to me," he says, with a laugh, "as the biggest Little Leaguer of them all. But outside of that it was no big thing. The program was still pretty new then.

"I did have a story ghost written under my name once, and some of my comments were blown a little out of proportion. I said I thought the program was very worth while, but what made it harmful in some cases was the parental interference and, occasionally, a manager who vicariously tries to be Casey Stengel or Leo Durocher. Of course, that isn't the program's fault. It's just people.

"A national magazine followed it up with a story, again over my name, and it had my consent. But they added a whole bunch of material to it, supposedly true incidents involving cases of overemphasis by the parents. They were things I had no way of knowing about. I got some letters on that, pro and con.

"But I feel very fortunate to have had the opportunity to have played at that age. It had a good influence on me. Even today Bernie O'Rourke, who started the program in Middletown, is a good friend of mine. We keep in touch at Christmas and I think he had something to do with naming one of the Little League teams after me back home. I have fond memories of it. I went to school with most of my teammates and we were close. I can still remember some of the games, and I remember where I hit the homer that won the all-star game. It was a line drive that went over the second baseman's head, bounced between the center and right fielder and kept rolling. At that time we didn't have fences, and the ball just rolled forever."

So do the memories of our youth roll on, forever, like Joey Jay's all-star homer. Today he's in the oil business in Charleston, West Va., the father of a teenage son, Steve, who is a second generation kid baseball product. And the name still catches the ear.

Joey Jay laughed. "I have to make a lot of contacts in the oil business," he said. "I tell them the name and you can see them straining their brain, trying to remember where they heard it."

There is just a trace of Jack Nicklaus in the face of John (Boog) Powell. It must be all that blondness, the blue eyes, the ivory skin, the smile. It's like looking directly into the sun. The voice, like Jack's, is gentle and somewhat thin, a bit of a surprise coming out of all that heft.

The voice was rendered speechless in August of 1954 when twelve-year-old Boog Powell, pitching for the Lakeland (Florida) team in the first round of the Little League World Series, established a record that was still standing twenty years later. He allowed the Schenectady (New York) team a total of 15 runs in three innings. It seems hardly worth noting that Lakeland lost, 16-0.

The experience was hardly the trauma that it appears on the surface, however. The fact is that young Boog was speechless *before* the game was even played. He had laryngitis and a bad case of the punies, not to mention the fact that he had pitched in six out of seven games to get his team out of Florida, and in two out of three to pull them through the regionals at Greensboro, N.C. Notwithstanding all that, Boog gave his all at Williamsport, and Schenectady took it.

TRIM

" NICE SLIDE, BERNIE. "

Of course, the handicap of losing one's voice isn't easily measured. After all, except for an occasional visit by his catcher, to whom can a pitcher talk? The rosin bag? But for a pure, psychological *curse* what could be worse to a twelve-year-old boy than to be struck silent during the most exciting week of his life?

Boog Powell looks back on that week not in anger or

embarrassment, but with a sort of reverse pride in the *size* of the calamity that befell him. This was no ordinary sinking. It was the *Titanic*. "The laryngitis bothered me," he says, "and I had pitched all those games, and the roof just caved in. One thing I remember very clearly, I gave up the only home run that ever cleared the dike behind the old ball park. It was like 300 feet to the fence, and there

" ROLLO'S WORKING ON A NEW PITCH. IT'S CALLED A STRIKE!"

was this 60-foot dike behind it, and a kid named Bill Mazuche hit one over the whole thing. I mean, it was a big league poke. From an aesthetic point of view, I had to admire it."

As luck would have it, when Boog and the Baltimore Orioles reached the World Series of 1966, he encountered Jim Barbieri, a reserve outfielder for the Dodgers who had played on that winning Schenectady team at Williamsport in '54. Powell had the distinction of being the first player to *start* in both classics. But the presence of Barbieri meant that two Little League finalists from the same tourney were to be represented in the adult World Series, a coincidence that would defy the odds of Jimmy the Greek.

"We stood and talked about it for fifteen minutes or so before the opening game," says Boog, "me and Jim. We talked about what it had been like, and what the guys we both knew were doing now. Mostly, what I remembered about it was Bill Mazuche and the home run he hit. Naturally, it was off my fast ball. That's all we threw. Just rare back and let it go. I had a curve ball and some other stuff, like most of the other kids, but nobody could throw any of it for a strike.

"You know, it was quite an experience for a twelve-year old kid. We got up there and they had rooms for us at Lycoming College. None of us kids from Florida even knew how to wear sanitaries. We were wearing black, high-topped tennis shoes, with the white shoelaces. They gave us brand new Little League spikes and all kind of new gear to play in.

"It's funny, but I thought about it in 1966, when we took the field to play the Dodgers. I was really excited. It was something you had worked for all your life. You had come to a point in your career where you could say, yes, *this is it.* And then I realized, it wasn't much different from what I had felt in 1954. I went out there, I was so nervous, I had the same butterflies I felt later in the '66 Series. It was just the same thing. It was what we had been working for. If anything, the pressure was greater on you at the Little League series. It was single elimination, one loss and you're out. We had come all that way, won all those games just to get out of Florida, and now you lose one and you're finished. The pressure was really heavy.

"When we lost, the initial shock passed quickly. After the game we cracked up, of course. Everybody cried a little. But kids recover fast. The main thing was, they let us stay for the rest of the tournament. We visited the river and an amusement park and just had a ball. Even when we got back home to Lakeland, the band was there, and the mayor, and the next day we were on the front page of the newspaper, with a photograph of us getting off the train. It was a great feeling, even though we had lost."

Part of the feeling was knowing that it was all in the family. Boog's older brother, Charley, played right field, and his half-brother, Carl Taylor (who made it to the big leagues as a utilityman) was the catcher. "My dad and stepmother took care of the team's travel details and uniforms," remembers Boog. "For four years our whole life revolved around it, around the Little League scene. We all got a lot out of it."

Boog pitched for the usual reason: he was the biggest and strongest kid on the team. He might have remained a pitcher except for an accident the next year that changed his career planning, "I was in junior high, playing third base one day," he says, "and we were charging ground balls during infield drill. I made a throw to first and something in my arm just went. For about the next two years I couldn't throw the ball across the diamond. When I got to high school, as a sophomore, they made me a catcher, but I still had trouble throwing. It wasn't until my junior year that my arm started to come around. By then I was an outfielder. I signed with Baltimore as an outfielder, and I played there my first four years in the big leagues."

That was mainly for the convenience of the Orioles, who had to accomodate Diamond Jim Gentile and Norm Siebern at first base. By 1966 both were gone, and Powell moved to what everyone agreed was his natural position. At six feet, four inches and 250 pounds, he made a perfect anchorman for the Baltimore infield.

In his first full season at first base, Boog socked 34 homers and drove in 109 runs to lead a Baltimore team best known for its pitching and defense. Behind the arms of Dave McNally (two wins), Jim Palmer and Wally Bunker (one each), the Orioles blitzed the Dodgers in four straight games, the last three by shutouts. It was a truly surgical performance. Virtually unnoticed was the fact that Boog Powell, at .357, was the only Baltimore player to bat over .300.

This has been one of the ironies of his distinguished big league career. He established himself in Baltimore lore as the first player to hit 300 homers and drive in 1,000 runs. He was the all star first baseman three times and, in 1970, the American League's most valuable player.

And yet Boog seemed always overshadowed by the brilliant glove and clutch instincts of Brooks Robinson, or the skills and leadership of Frank Robinson, or the dazzle of a line of splendid young pitchers. When he encountered a distressing slump early in the 1974 season, Boog grinned and said, half-seriously, "This will pass soon and then everybody can ignore me like they always did before."

Not always, of course. Since the age of twelve Boog has been doing it for the record, and for the fans who admire effort. The ball may, as Baltimore observers noted long ago, travel three miles or three feet, but Boog Powell always took a full cut. Even on the day of his great adversity, in 1954, at Williamsport, he moved to shortstop and hit safely twice.

Coincidentally, John Powell, Jr., at the age of eleven, was playing Little League baseball for the Eastwood A's in Baltimore, in the summer of 1974. When he wasn't pitching, he played first base. Shades of Pop.

In fact, if the program needed a kind of living testimonial, what could be better than to note that Steve Jay and John Powell, Jr., both followed their fathers into kid baseball, carrying on the legend of the greatest little game's two earliest achievers.

8. The Great Teams

Mexico and Taiwan,
Who Put "World" into the World Series

The Little League World Series had become the show-piece of all kid baseball. It was more than just a dream game for those who play and those who coach and root and drive the car pool. It was an international happening, unlike its big league counterpart. For years Europeans have laughed at the conceit of Americans, who can casually refer to a tournament between, say, Los Angeles and Oakland, as being the *world championship*. But not at Williamsport, where teams like Monterrey and Taiwan had proved that it's a small world, after all.

Of course, all that has changed, now. Tired of being beat at their own game, Little League officials decided, in November, 1974 to take the "world" out of the world championship. The kids who play the game may be less for it. The game, itself, may be less for it. But the memories remain of those brilliant teams from Mexico and Taiwan— and of those kids whose mastery of kid baseball was unparalleled.

As the final game of the 1958 Little League Series came down to two outs in the final inning, Mexico had a 10-1 lead over Kankakee, Illinois.

Mexico's pitcher, a towering (5-6) beanpole named Hector Torres, walked halfway in from the mound, doffed his cap and bowed low to his catcher, Carlos Trevino.

"*Te dedico este bateador*" Torres said to Trevino. The batter, Joe Wichnowski, didn't know he had been insulted, because he didn't understand Spanish: "I dedicate this batter to you."

The only thing Torres didn't do was turn his back and fling his cap over his shoulder to a señorita in the grandstand. But he dispatched Wichnowski with three straight strikes, and the kids from Monterrey had completed the impossible—back to back Little League world championships. It had seemed impossible enough the year before, when fourteen ragtag midgets from South of the Border had captured American hearts by sweeping thirteen bigger foes aside on their way to the most glorious title in boys' baseball.

Now Monterrey, which had produced the miracle team of 1957, had done it again, perhaps knocking down the going value of miracles. Monterrey had done it with an almost completely new team. Only one player on the squad had been at Williamsport the summer before.

In all the years of Little League competition, two victors stand out as the greatest of them all—the Monterrey Chamacos and the Taiwan Giants of the Chinese Republic. Surely there were other Little League champions of other years who were the equal or perhaps superior to this pair of storied entries. But aside from the expert way in which they dispatched all opponents, the Mexicans and the Chinese accomplished something *extra* for the prestige of the Williamsport classic.

It has been forever a source of amusement to foreign sports fans that American professional baseball annually conducts a "World Series." An English soccer writer, Brian Glanville of London, was covering the sport's World Cup in Mexico in 1970 and remarked about the baseball plan: "It's very quaint. One team in the United States plays

by Jeff Millar & Bill Hinds

another team in the United States and is declared 'World' champion. We used to call the game 'rounders,' you know."

Perhaps that is the reason the national media, particularly the newspapers, magazines and television networks, reacted so explosively to the first invasion from Monterrey. It was a victory for the "littlest" of the little people (the players averaged 4-11 and 92 pounds), but it was also a victory for the World out there, and it made the Williamsport title the most legitimate international crown this side of the Olympics and the World Cup of B. Glanville, Esq.

They were a hard group to resist, that first Monterrey team. This was not a Cinderella afraid the coach-and-four would turn into pumpkin-and-mice. The Chamacos rode a pumpkin all the way. To begin with, they were recruited from the factory area of Monterrey, where the going wage was $1.50 per day. There were only four teams in the league, a small number to produce such a wealth of talent.

Monterrey's youngsters regarded it as highest adventure to go north to McAllen, Texas, for the district playoffs. Most of them had never been to downtown Monterrey! They were paired in the opening game of the four-team tournament against the mighty fellows of Mexico City. A victory in that one would make Monterrey champions of all Mexico, a great enough goal. "Don't those big kids from Mexico City scare you?" a Texan asked second baseman Pini Gonzales at the hotel coffee shop. Pini's answer was big league. "We don't have to *carry* them," he said, "just play them." Pini had learned to speak a little Americano shining shoes for American tourists.

The Monterrey manager, Cesar Faz, was born in Texas and had been batboy with the San Antonio Missions of the Texas League and later with the St. Louis Browns in the American League. He schooled his youngsters in all the niceties of big league play, including a studied air of calm assurance during pregame practice, to unsettle the opposition. He was also something of a psychologist. When his charges rebelled against taking their usual pregame siesta, because they could see their opponents of the afternoon frolicking in the motel swimming pool, Faz said, "All right, those who want to win today's game will go to bed. The others may go swimming." That ended the protests.

Monterrey brushed aside Mexico City, defeated the home McAllen team with equal ease, and on the third day introduced its amazing pitcher, Angel Macias. Macias was more than a pitcher. He was a righthanded shortstop, a lefthanded first baseman—and a pitcher who could throw with either hand! He held Mission, Texas, to one hit, and Monterrey was the champion of the tournament, advancing to next week's district round, also at McAllen. But the team only had $3 left in its expense fund. All they had planned to do was beat Mexico City and go home. Certainly they couldn't defeat the Texas gringos at their own game.

Two McAllen ranchers, who appreciated good baseball whenever they saw it, took over the motel bill. A cafe owner cut his prices for team meals, and McAllen citizens took turns inviting the team to home-cooked meals. The newspapers hailed them as *"chamacos maravillos,"* the wonder kids.

Monterrey brushed aside its next pair of Texas teams,

Weslaco and Brownsville, with equal ease. When Macias hurled the final strike past a Brownsville batter, he ran to Manager Faz and said, *"Now,* can we go swimming?"

The newfound McAllen fans followed the team to the sectional playoffs at Corpus Christi (two more wins) and some even went to Fort Worth to see Monterrey win the

" YOU'RE OUT....UNLESS I MISS MY GUESS."

Texas state championship. Expenses were now coming from the tournament profits at the gate, and the boys were treated to their first airplane ride, a trip to the southern regional tournament at Louisville, Kentucky. Their traveling wardrobes were not much when they left home and now were somewhere between threadbare and ragged. A Louisville merchant, one of the Little League fans who turned out to greet incoming teams at the airport, saw them get off the plane and said, "The champions of Texas deserve to look better than that." He outfitted the whole team with new clothes, gratis.

The attention from newsreel men and autograph seekers had unnerved the youngsters, and they were clearly not themselves in the first three innings of a scoreless game against Biloxi, Mississippi. Harold Haskins, the man who started the Little League program in Monterrey and had stayed with his champs all the way, thought he knew how

"TIE!"

to jolt them awake. Haskins played a phonograph record over the park's loudspeakers. As "Corrido de Monterrey" blared forth, the dugout was filled with laughter and smiles. The *chamacos* loaded the bases and Pepe Maiz cleared them with a grand slam homer. Then Macias pitched another one-hitter to whip Owensboro, Kentucky, and Monterrey finally had its ticket to Williamsport.

By this time the city of Monterrey had come awake, too, realizing it had something special conquering its way across the United States. Before the opening game at Williamsport, the Mexican flag was raised to the tune of the national anthem, diplomats from Washington, D.C., and New York were in the stands, beside the Monterrey mayor and city treasurer.

The Bridgeport, Connecticut, opponent was tougher than any Monterrey had faced before—but when the Bridgeport shortstop made a putout at second and kept his back turned too long, Fidel Ruiz stole home with the winning run for a 2-1 victory.

In the final game, it looked like a set of Davids matched against Goliaths. The LaMesa, California, team averaged 5-4 and 127 pounds—which meant that Monterrey was giving away five inches at height and 35 pounds per player. A classic performance was demanded, and Angel Macias delivered it. As Don Larsen had done for the New York Yankees the previous October, Macias pitched a perfect game. Nobody reached first, nobody hit a ball out of the infield and Macias struck out 11.

Back home in Monterrey, the citizens had a formula for celebration. It is described in the Spanish phrase, *echar la casa por la ventana*, "to throw the house out the window." This Monterrey proceeded to do, to the tune of fire sirens, factory whistles, church bells and fireworks.

The World Champions were not yet through their American Odyssey. They went to New York and met the Brooklyn Dodgers and the visiting St. Louis Cardinals. Then on to Washington where the President presented each with a fountain pen inscribed, "Stolen from Dwight D. Eisenhower."

The following year's repeat victory, led by pitcher Torres, who had never played baseball until that season began, was almost an anticlimax, except that it proved the first championship was no fluke.

For most of the youngsters, this had been the finest hour of their lives. Torres later signed with the Houston Astros as a shortstop and played parts of seven seasons in the major leagues. His catcher, nicknamed "Bobby" Trevino, had seventeen games with the California Angels. Another Angel, Macias, had a trial with the Los Angeles Dodgers farm system but never made it.

None would ever forget, however, the two years when Monterrey ruled the world of kid baseball.

"I HEAR THEY'RE SCORING A LOT OF RUNS LATELY."

Thereafter—through 1966—U.S. teams would prevail, temporarily saving the national honor and, as events soon proved, lulling us into a sense of false complacency. In a remarkable run of success, the Far East produced seven World Series champions in the next eight years. Puzzled

Americans might well have echoed the immortal words of Casey Stengel: "Can't anybody here play this game (anymore)?"

Since West Tokyo first won in 1967, it had become evident that more World Championship games were played in the Orient than at Williamsport—when the Taiwan champion met the Japanese champion. Only in 1970, when Wayne (New Jersey) won an all-U.S. final over Campbell (California), was there a breakthrough by Occidentals.

Then came the three-year streak by the kids from Taiwan, who brought a whole new scene to the World Series. Their fans flocked to Williamsport by the thousands, decked out in colorful national dress, waving flags and banging gongs—big gongs and small gongs, the kind that make your teeth vibrate. The Chinese Republic's ambassador to the U.S. sent his chef to Williamsport to prepare the food for the young heroes, something about American food being filling, and all that, but an hour later you need Alka Seltzer. (Their meals consisted mainly of rice, noodles and chicken and, to the delight of their American hosts, they ate nearly everything with chopsticks.)

The Taiwan lads brought something else with them— good, old-fashioned, international controversy. After the 1973 World Series, in which Taiwan held three opponents runless and hitless and won by a combined score of 57-0, the howls could be heard from here to, well, China. Rumors spread that the Chinese players were over the Little League age limit of twelve. You don't get *that* inscrutable in eleven years, do you? Maybe the Chinese didn't count the Year of the Tiger in computing their children's ages. Maybe thirteen was an unlucky number in Chinese, so their kids stayed at age twelve for twenty-four months.

And even if they were a legit twelve, who knows what other Little League rules the Chinese were skirting? Suspicious U.S. coaches pointed out that their teams were survivors of local tournaments. That is, the players were selected from a comparatively small group. But suppose Taiwan was getting up an All-Star team from a field of two million? It would be like picking the best players from the state of California and entering them as a unit. They, too, would be unbeatable.

So, to answer all the charges, the Little League headquarters dispatched two emissaries to visit Taiwan after the '73 tournament and examine the leagues over there in detail. The answers were simple and not at all devious. The kids were the correct age, and they were not a select squad from myriad entries. Taiwan has only twenty-three leagues, originating out of the school prefectures. Team boundaries were similar in size to the U.S. entrants. The big differences were two: Baseball was the *only* sport played in Taiwan, played, in fact, year-round in two-hour daily sessions. And, the boys received excellent professional coaching from the athletic staffs of the upper-grade (high) schools.

Taiwan was winning every year for a reason basic to the sport: they practiced baseball more, and practice made perfect. The only result of the investigation was that Taiwan Little League officials agreed not to use professional school coaches to prepare the teams.

Actually, if anyone had been listening, a spokesman for the Taiwan Little League had offered the perfect rebuttal to charges that their players were over the age limit. Since the young men of his country face a compulsory draft at eighteen, he said, the record of birth "is a very serious matter." In short, they don't fudge.

A whole swarm of stereotypes went out the window when this small island country, better known as Nationalist China, began to dominate the Little League World Series. From their culture we adopted fortune cookies, firecrackers and hand laundries, but we never expected them to beat us at our own game.

It came as a bit of a shock to discover that their kids were bigger than ours. Out of a roster of fourteen players, the 1973 Taiwan team had twelve who weighed 100

TRIM

" REALLY DIGS IN, DOESN'T HE? "

pounds or over, and thirteen who stood taller than 5 feet. And how they played the game!

Taiwan's dominance in the world championship became so complete that the president of its baseball association, Hsieh Kuo-cheng, could only apologize. "I am sorry. We were too strong," making the rounds from victim to victim.

But Hsieh need have no apologies for the *way* Taiwan climbed to the pinnacle of kid baseball. He can recall twenty postwar years when the island's teams competed on a marked-off city lot, when there was so little money to finance the game that the kids had to play with rubber baseballs and sticks for bats.

It was the mountain village of Red Leaf that started Taiwan on the way to international glory. When the Red

Leaf champions induced a visiting Japanese team to play them a game using the rubber ball, the result was no contest. The visitors left behind a dozen baseballs and a suggestion that Red Leaf should try the real game. A year later Taiwan scored the first of its triumphs at Williamsport.

A member of that first team, third baseman Yu Hung-kai, also was later a member of the Senior League team (age thirteen-fifteen) that won championships at Gary, Indiana. His prowess was rewarded with a scholarship to the island's elite Huahsing school. Yu recalls the long road of sacrifice that lead down the mountain from Red Leaf. "We would get up at five in the morning to play a game before school. Sometimes we'd just forget about school and play straight through the day. We still practice every day except for some days in winter. Every day I get about forty swings in batting practice and they hit about forty balls to each outfielder and forty grounders to the infielders. If you make errors, they might hit you eighty balls."

Almost as overwhelming as the quality of their baseball was Taiwan's display of manners. American crowds are simply not prepared for such Oriental courtesies as bowing to the umpire before hitting. They also bow and tip their caps to the crowd, and at the start of each game the team ran onto the field in a single line, circled home plate and first base and met in a huddle on the pitcher's mound.

They were a smiling, graceful lot who played with great seriousness and great dignity. Off the field they seemed to have a better time than anyone, and it is a pity that the language barrier did not allow for a closer study. The

Taiwan players told interviewers, through an interpreter, that American names were hard to pronounce.

Clearly, the good news they kept sending back home each August was well and widely received. In 1969, when Taipei shut out California to start it all, the championship game was telecast back to Taiwan via satellite. An estimated eight million Chinese watched the game, live, at 2 A.M.

After that the Taiwan teams alternated—Tainan in 1971, '73 and '74. Taipei again in 1972. But with measured Oriental aplomb, they suggested that national chauvinism was not involved. "It has no relationship to national honor," said the team interpreter, Kang Shau-Ho. "It is team honor and personal honor, because they want to make new records."

Records are perishable, of course, but the teams from the Republic of China have left a lasting impression on the fans and players of kid baseball. They have given us a lesson in baseball and geography, in understanding and human relations. The Little League has tried to set aside that lesson by banning foreign competition. But kid baseball is too popular a sport to remain within our own borders. It's appeal is world-wide, which is to be expected from the greatest little game.

Mickey Herskowitz and Steve Perkins are a nationally known Texas writing team and coauthors of the syndicated column *Sports Hot Line*. They have collaborated on several books including a biography of Jimmy ("The Greek") Snyder.

Herskowitz assisted Howard Cosell with the writing of his best-selling biography *Cosell*. He covered major league baseball on a daily basis for five years and was the 1970 winner of the National Headliner's Award for sportswriting.

Perkins has twenty-three years' experience as a sportswriter in both professional baseball and football. Eight of those years was spent covering the Dallas Cowboys including their Super Bowl victory in 1972. Some of his published works include *Next Year's Champions* and *Winning the Big One*. He himself is the father of two kid baseball players.